Keto Meal Prep For Beginners 2019

Fast and Easy Recipes For Weight Loss and Healthy Eating and Lose 20 Pounds In 3 Weeks

By
Dr Emma Walker

Table of Content

Chapter 4 Dinner Recipes 56

21 Days Meal Plan for Meal Prep 89

Chapter 1 Keto Meal Prep

The Benefits of Meal Prep

Saves money: Due to the fact that meal preps would have you outline everything you would eat over a certain period of time, you get to buy food items in bulk and you buy them once, this saved a lot of money for me.

Weight loss: Meal prep allows you the opportunity to eat the right foods at the right time and at the right calorie. This simply means you would enter ketosis much faster thereby granting you the weight loss you so desire much faster.

Time saver: In truth, before I started with a proper meal prep, I often spent loads and loads of time thinking of what would be appropriate for me to eat. It really took my time and then I could start preparing one dish and suddenly lose interest in it but with the meal prep, everything is outlined properly and I didn't have to waste time selecting a particular food from various options.

Stress reduction: I do not really know about anyone else, but the meal prep really helped reduce my stress level by far this was because I no longer needed to make regular trips to the store as much as I usually did before and the meal prep allowed me calculate the number of calories for each food taken, this reduced the stress of calculating every time right before I ate a meal.

Easy grocery shopping: The keto meal prep makes shopping for groceries really easy, this is because you know exactly what you want and need and it also doesn't allow you go overboard especially when you are a carbohydrate lover and might want to pick a few of your favorite carbohydrate food, the meal prep limits you.

Less waste: Thanks to the meal prep, food wastage is reduced because every single food item you buy is needed for the meal to be prepared, this to a great extent reduces wastage.

The Keto Diet Macros

Fats: The peculiar thing about keto diet is that it actually encourages you to up on your fat intake and so you would need to eat foods considerably high in fats, it's important to note that not all fats are considered healthy and you must be picky about the kind of fat you eat, because unhealthy fats just cause a build up to your cholesterol level and leave you in a worst state than you were when you started the diet. Saturated fats are without doubt the best, they are healthy and would help you achieve into ketosis faster because they are easily oxidized to energy quickly.

Protein: Your protein intake at best should be moderate, it should never for any reason be higher in your body than fats this is because your body is still capable of using protein instead of fats for energy and when this happens, you wouldn't be losing weight, you would be topping up the tank.

Carbohydrates: You must understand this part of the whole process for this to work. Your carbs intake must be greatly reduced; this should be done to achieve the state of ketosis that would provide a lot of benefits. You may not fully need to cut down on carbs entirely but you do have to reduce it to a level that would almost be insignificant. At first, I tried cutting them off entirely but the keto-flu hit me really hard and Nate advised me to up my carbs intake for a while in a bid to allow the change in diet a lot easier for my body. Change is gradual!

Supplements: Obviously, this is not a nutrient but along the line you would soon discover that while the keto diet is healthy, you would still need to stock on some supplements that would replace some of the kind of foods that you are not allowed to eat for the duration of the diet.

Prep for Your Kitchen

Stocking your kitchen:

You have got to be battle ready for keto dieting and by battle ready I mean that you should get all that you would possibly need. When I started out the diet, a really helpful factor was a fully stocked kitchen. I didn't have to make short trips to go the grocery store for certain ingredients I might need to prepare the meal for the day because all I could possibly need to make my keto diet a success was right there in my kitchen and so I had no excuse to slack off with the diet and this applies for other keto beginners, a fully stocked kitchen would always help to keep you on the right track with the goal in sight.

Meal prepping equipment:

A lot of people complain about keto diet saying it's quite hard to keep up, I felt the same way at first, then I did a thorough research on the area and found out about some equipment that would really help me throughout the process. In truth, my keto meal prep would not be without some of these equipment:

Slow cooker: I'm pretty sure that literally everyone is familiar with a slow cooker and even has one in their homes I don't know if I have said this before but I am a bold and proud meat lover and so the slow cooker was a really valuable equipment to my cause because it helped me cook large quantities of meat and I basically had to do nothing but wait till it's done and enjoy the meaty treat plus it's the best equipment to bring out the flavor in various kinds of meats.

Spiralizer: For us keto dieter, spiralizers are key for our success especially for foods like noodles which are like everyone's personal favorite. The spiralizer reduces to a very insignificant amount the carbohydrate in foods like noodles.

Water bottle: Due to the fact that starting off the keto diet would get you low on water and other electrolytes, a water bottle would come in handy for you. Mine had a stylish band I could fit my hand in, it was really helpful because I was always finding myself to be dehydrated.

Automated slicer: Your keto prep kitchen would not be complete without your automated slicer, it slices eggs, avocados, cheese and so on in sizeable chunks hat are perfect for eating just as they are or for using them to prepare various keto friendly delicacies.

Kitchen scale: I am pretty sure that I do to need to over emphasize on the importance of owning a kitchen scale for a person who wants to succeed in keto dieting. For me, it was an irreplaceable tool for my keto meal prep, it helped me measure the ingredients and groceries I used to prepare my keto meals. This ensured that I never went overboard for any delicacy. I tracked my calorie intake and ensured I took just the right amount of foods to prevent any mishaps.

Blender: Whether it's for making keto friendly smoothies or for preparing those creamy soups we all love; a blender is a very important equipment for your keto meal prep. To be honest, I was never really a fan of soups and so I used my blender specifically to make avocado smoothies. Avocados as we all know are an important addition to the keto meal prep plus they make for really tasty smoothies. If you doubt me, try it out!

Non-stick frying pan: This was a tool of immeasurable value for me because I loved my fried foods and a non-stick frying pan is a really healthy way to enjoy them. It is perfect for making all those keto-friendly pancakes and those extra crunchy keto chips.

Automated vegetable chopper: I hated chopping vegetables and the worst of them all for me was onions, I loved eating them but it's the chopping part of the whole process that kills me every time and so the automated chopper chops all my veggies for me in no time, it's a really helpful tool when you want to make those low carb keto friendly salads.

Ketone test strips: This isn't exactly an equipment but I thought to add it here for the meal prep because it really helped me to track my ketone levels which is why I could add it to the list of keto meal prep tools. I mean, you never know how far you have progressed or if you have even progressed at all if you do not check your ketone level. The most appealing thing about this test kit is that you can carry out the test right there in the comfort of your home and it was better than having to go to the clinic to get tested. For me, it was a hassle to go regularly to check my ketone levels but with the test kit, you don't have to stress at all and you can check your ketone levels anytime, any day.

Milk frother: You can make all the whipped cream you want with this equipment, it's also excellent for mixing your keto friendly coffee ingredients to make your morning mix. I made my favorite lattes with this equipment, just what I need to perk me up for the day ahead.

Step-by-Step to Start Meal Prep

I'm going to give a very simple outline on the steps I carried out to make my keto meal prep a smashing success and I hope you find it to be useful.

Step 1: Make a shopping list.

To do this, you would need to acquaint yourself with the keto friendly foods available, this would enable you create a shopping list that would perfectly suit your lifestyle as well as your taste buds. Of course, if you are a bit too low on funds, I do not need to tell you that the shopping list has to be economic friendly. My point is, just because it's a keto meal prep, it doesn't mean it must be extravagant.

Step 2: Go shopping

I'm pretty sure I do not need to say much on this. When shopping, I usually liked eating something crunchy, it's kind of like my quirk and I know lots of people have other quirks. So, if you have a habit of eating crunchy foods like chips amongst many others while shopping, it's better to go for the keto friendly snacks. Believe me, there are a whole lot of them. Also, it's important to appropriately check the brand of foods you buy as a couple of brands sell fatty foods, cheese and other items with low quality which would do you more harm than good.

Step 3: Start with a clean area

One of the best sayings I ever heard was clear your mind, see only the task that is and it's the same for meal prepping. By clean area I do not just mean for you to sweep and clean up your kitchen and working area. Staring out keto dieting is a bit like going to war and as such, you would need to get rid of obstacles that might get in your way of success. Here, carbohydrate is the enemy and so if you love carbs, it better to take them all away from your line of sight to prevent you from going back to them in no time. If you clear out every obstacle, then without a doubt you can probably focus.

Step 4: Start cooking

After all the preparations are completed, you do have to get to work. Apart from getting the right groceries to prepare your keto meals, you should also note that there is a certain kind of way these foods should be cooked to ensure that you are enriched with the optimal amount of nutrients you would need. With the right equipment and with the right recipe, cooking shouldn't be a problem for you. I mean, if a klutz like myself could safely prepare my keto meals, then you definitely can.

Top 3 Important Tips for Keto Prep

Always supplement:

Even though the keto diet it is very healthy, it still has some lacking nutrients, which is the reason you would have to add supplements, they would help you get the most out of the whole process. Supplements are also advised because they help out with the keto-flu plus they also help you regain electrolytes that you are most likely to lose during the process. You would need to put stuff like MCT oil in your foods or even in your morning coffee every once in a while. Also, I thought you should know that at the beginning of the diet, you would lose a lot of weight, most of this is water weight and due to this loss, you would often find yourself feeling dehydrated. So, in this case water is a very good supplement. Drink as much as you can to replenish lost body water.

Exercise:

Exercising and keto diet are likened to two peas in a pod, keto diet is much more effective with exercise. As said before, exercises are very helpful because they help you achieve ketosis way faster because your glucose stores deplete way faster thanks to exercises. If you have been doing exercises before, you might be feeling a bit weaker than usual and you might also find it unable to work out as much as you usually did but you do not need to fret as it is a normal sign as your body adjusts to the changes in diet. So, if this happens, you do not need to over exert yourself, a little rest once in a while would do you no harm and you can take things easy till your normal energy level kicks back in and thanks to ketosis, it would even be more than it had been before.

Never run out of stock:

A study explained that it was really easy for people on the keto diet to go back to eating their usual carbs rich food. It's likely you run out of the ingredients and foodstuff required to make your keto meals and you just look into the fridge and decide to indulge a little with your chicken nuggets marinated in sugary sauce or something like that. You might keep procrastinating your trip to the grocery store and just like that you get back to your old habit of eating carbohydrate rich foods. For this reason, thanks to the meal prep, you know what exactly you are required to eat for each day and this would provide you with the avenue to stock up on what you would need to make these dishes and before you completely run out, you could always get more.

Some Money Saving Tips

Buy in bulk: Buying groceries in bulk has with it a whole lot of advantages, one of them include the fact that it is way cheaper than buying in single pieces plus you save yourself the stress of making repeated trips to the store to get one thing or the other. If your kitchen is fully stocked, your keto meal prepping would be nothing but a smashing success.

Shop local: Rather than shopping for my food items from online stores where I may or may not be sure of the quality of the foods, I preferred to take the trips to the stores myself allowing me the opportunity to gauge the freshness of the food items.

Chapter 2 Breakfast Recipes

Satisfying Breakfast Smoothie

Serves: 2

Preparation Time: 10 minutes

Ingredients:

- 2 scoops unsweetened whey protein powder
- 4 tbsp. heavy cream
- ½ tsp. ground cinnamon
- 6-8 drops liquid stevia
- ¾ C. coffee
- 1½ C. unsweetened coconut milk
- ½ C. ice cubes

Instructions:

1) In a high-speed blender, add all the ingredients and pulse until smooth.
2) Transfer into 2 serving glasses and serve immediately.

Nutrition Information:

Calories per serving: 392; Carbohydrates: 6.2g; Protein: 24.3g; Fat: 28.9g; Sugar: 4g; Sodium: 100mg; Fiber: 0.3g

Protein Rich Smoothie

Serves: 2

Preparation Time: 5 minutes

Ingredients:

- 1½ scoops unsweetened protein powder
- 2 tbsp. cacao powder
- 2 tbsp. unsweetened peanut butter
- 8-10 drops liquid stevia
- Pinch of salt
- 1½ C. unsweetened coconut milk
- ¼ C. ice cubes

Instructions:

1) In a high-speed blender, add all the ingredients and pulse until smooth.
2) Transfer into 2 serving glasses and serve immediately.

Nutrition Information:

Calories per serving: 460; Carbohydrates: 9g; Protein: 25.3g; Fat: 34.5g; Sugar: 5g; Sodium: 332mg; Fiber: 2.5g

Healthy Breakfast Cereal

Serves: 12

Preparation Time: 15 minutes, Cooking Time: 40 minutes

Ingredients:

- 1 C. unsweetened coconut, shredded
- ½ C. almonds flakes
- ½ C. flax seeds
- 1/3 C. sunflower seeds
- 1/3 C. chia seeds
- 1/3 C. pumpkin seeds
- 1/3 C. Erythritol
- 1 tbsp. ground cinnamon
- 1/3 C. coconut oil, melted
- 1 tsp. organic vanilla extract

Instructions:

1) Preheat the oven to 320 degrees F. Line a baking sheet with parchment paper.
2) In a bowl, add all the ingredients and mix until well combined.
3) Transfer the mixture onto the prepared baking sheet and spread in an even layer.
4) Bake for about 30-40 minutes, stirring after every 5 minutes.
5) Remove from the oven and set aside to cool completely before serving.
6) You can enjoy this cereal with any non-dairy milk and your favorite berries topping.

Nutrition Information:

Calories per serving: 167; Carbohydrates: 6g; Protein: 3.8g; Fat: 15.3g; Sugar: 0.8g; Sodium: 4mg; Fiber: 4g

Best Homemade Granola

Serves: 15

Preparation Time: 15 minutes, Cooking Time: 50 minutes

Ingredients:

- 1/3 C. sesame seeds, toasted lightly
- 8 tbsp. Swerve
- ½ tsp. ground cinnamon
- ¾ C. pecans
- ¾ C. almonds, toasted lightly
- ½ C. pumpkin seeds, toasted lightly
- ½ C. sunflower seeds, toasted lightly
- ½ C. chia seeds
- ¼ C. flax seeds
- 2 organic egg whites
- Salt, to taste

Instructions:

1) Preheat the oven to 250 degrees F. Line a large rimmed baking sheet with parchment paper.
2) In a food processor, add the sesame seeds, Swerve and cinnamon and pulse until powdered.
3) Ina large bowl, add the sesame seeds mixture and remaining ingredients except the egg whites and mix until well combined.
4) Ina clean glass bowl, add the egg whites and salt and with an electric mixer, beat until soft peaks form.
5) Gently, fold the whipped egg whites into the nuts mixture.

6) Transfer the mixture onto the prepared baking sheet and spread in an even layer.

7) Sprinkle the granola with salt evenly.

8) Bake for about 45-50 minutes, stirring after every 15 minutes.

9) Remove from the oven and set aside to cool completely.

10) Break the granola in chunks and serve.

11) You can enjoy this granola with any non-dairy milk and your favorite berries topping.

Nutrition Information:

Calories per serving: 156; Carbohydrates: 7.2g; Protein: 5.4g; Fat: 13.5g; Sugar: 0.6g; Sodium: 66mg; Fiber: 3.9g

Fall Morning Porridge

Serves: 4

Preparation Time: 15 minutes, Cooking Time: 4 minutes

Ingredients:
- ¼ C. homemade pumpkin puree
- 1/3 C. almond flour
- 2 tbsp. coconut flour
- 2 tsp. ground flax seeds
- 2 tbsp. Erythritol
- ½ tsp. pumpkin pie spice
- ½ tsp. ground cinnamon
- ½ tsp. salt
- ¼ C. half-and-half
- ¾ C. water
- ¼ C. fresh strawberries, hulled and sliced

Instructions:
1) In a small pan, add all the ingredients except strawberry slices and with a wire whisk, beat until well combined.
2) Now, place the pan over medium heat and cook for about 3-4 minutes or until heated through, stirring continuously.
3) Remove from the heat and let it cool for about 5 minutes.
4) Transfer the porridge into serving bowls evenly.
5) Top with strawberry slices and serve.

Nutrition Information:
Calories per serving: 113; Carbohydrates: 8g; Protein: 3.7g; Fat: 7.6g; Sugar: 1g; Sodium: 303mg; Fiber: 3.8g

Overnight Porridge

Serves: 2

Preparation Time: 10 minutes

Ingredients:

- 2/3 C. plus ¼ C. unsweetened coconut milk, divided
- ½ C. hemp hearts
- 1 tbsp. chia seed
- 3-4 drops liquid stevia
- ½ tsp. organic vanilla extract
- Pinch of salt

Instructions:

1) In a larger airtight container, place 2/3 C. of the coconut milk, hemp hearts, chia seed, stevia, vanilla extract and salt and stir until well combined.
2) Cover the container tightly and refrigerate overnight.
3) Just before serving, add the remaining coconut milk and stir to combine.
4) Serve immediately.

Nutrition Information:

Calories per serving: 265; Carbohydrates: 6.5g; Protein: 14.1g; Fat: 20.4g; Sugar: 0.1g; Sodium: 78mg; Fiber: 5.7g

Eggy Flavored Crepes

Serves: 5

Preparation Time: 15 minutes, Cooking Time: 10 minutes

Ingredients:

- 6 oz. cream cheese, softened
- 1/3 C. Parmesan cheese, grated
- 6 large organic eggs
- 1 tsp. Erythritol
- 1½ tbsp. coconut flour
- 1/8 tsp. xanthan gum
- 2 tbsp. unsalted butter

Instructions:

1) In a blender, add the cream cheese, Parmesan cheese, eggs and Erythritol and pulse on low speed until well combined.
2) While the motor is running, place the coconut flour and xanthan gum and pulse until a thick mixture is formed.
3) Now, pulse on medium speed for about 5-10 seconds.
4) Transfer the mixture into a bowl and set aside for at least 5 minutes.
5) In a nonstick frying pan, melt the butter over medium-low heat.
6) Add ¼ C. of the mixture and tilt the pan to spread into a thin layer.
7) Cook for about 1½ minutes or until the edges become brown.
8) Carefully, flip the crepe and cook for about 15-20 seconds more.
9) Repeat with the remaining mixture.
10) Serve warm with your favorite keto friendly filling.

Nutrition Information:

Calories per serving: 283; Carbohydrates: 3.8g; Protein: 12.9g; Fat: 24.3g; Sugar: 0.8g; Sodium: 274mg; Fiber: 1.6g

Delicious Pancakes

Serves: 2

Preparation Time: 10 minutes, Cooking Time: 12 minutes

Ingredients:

- 7 oz. cottage cheese
- 2 organic eggs
- 1½ tbsp. psyllium husk

Instructions:

1) In a bowl, add all the ingredients and with a hand blender, mix until well combined.
2) Heat a greased skillet over me medium-low heat.
3) Add half of the mixture and tilt the pan to spread it in an even layer.
4) Cook for 2-3 minutes per side or until golden brown.
5) Flip the side and cook for about 1-2 minutes or until golden brown.
6) Repeat with the remaining mixture.
7) Serve warm.

Nutrition Information:

Calories per serving: 165; Carbohydrates: 7.7g; Protein: 19.2g; Fat: 6.3g; Sugar: 0.7g; Sodium: 468mg; Fiber: 3.4g

Nutrient Filled Pancakes

Serves: 8

Preparation Time: 15 minutes, Cooking Time: 56 minutes

Ingredients:

- 2 organic eggs
- 1 C. almond flour
- ½ tsp. organic baking powder
- ¼ C. water
- ½ C. feta cheese, crumbled
- 1 C. fresh spinach, chopped
- 2 scallions, chopped
- 1 garlic clove, chopped
- ¼ tsp. ground nutmeg
- Salt and ground black pepper, as required
- 2 tbsp. unsalted butter

Instructions:

1) In a bowl, crack the eggs and beat until frothy.
2) Add the almond flour, baking powder, and water and beat until smooth.
3) Add the feta cheese, spinach, scallions, garlic, nutmeg, salt and black pepper and stir to combine.
4) In a large nonstick frying pan, melt ½ tbsp. of the butter over medium heat.
5) Add desired amount of the mixture and tilt the pan to spread it in an even layer.
6) Cook for about 3-4 minutes or until golden brown.
7) Flip the side and cook for about 2-3 more minutes.
8) Repeat with the remaining butter and spinach mixture.
9) Serve warm.

Nutrition Information:

Calories per serving: 179; Carbohydrates: 4.3g; Protein: 6g; Fat: 15.6g; Sugar: 0.6g; Sodium: 317mg; Fiber: 1.7g

Authentic Belgian Waffles

Serves: 4

Preparation Time: 10 minutes, Cooking Time: 20 minutes

Ingredients:

- 8 oz. cream cheese, softened
- 5 large organic eggs (at room temperature)
- 1/3 C. coconut flour
- 2 tbsp. powdered Erythritol
- ½ tsp. xanthan gum
- ¼ tsp. baking soda
- ½ tsp. pumpkin pie spice
- Pinch of salt
- ½ tsp. organic vanilla extract
- ¼ tsp. organic almond extract
- 1/3 C. unsweetened almond milk

Instructions:

1) Preheat the waffle iron and lightly grease it.
2) In a food processor, add all the ingredients except the almond milk and pulse until smooth and creamy.
3) Transfer the mixture into a bowl.
4) Add the almond milk and with a spatula, mix until well combined.
5) Preheat the waffle iron and lightly grease it.
6) In a large bowl, add the flour and baking powder and mix well.
7) Add remaining ingredients and mix until well combined.
8) Place ¼ of the mixture in preheated waffle iron.
9) Cook for about 4-5 minutes or until waffles become golden brown.
10) Repeat with the remaining mixture.
11) Serve warm.

Nutrition Information:

Calories per serving: 335; Carbohydrates: 9.5g; Protein: 13.6g; Fat: 27.3g; Sugar: 0.7g; Sodium: 397mg; Fiber: 4.5g

Savory Herbed Waffles

Serves: 4

Preparation Time: 15 minutes, Cooking Time: 12 minutes

Ingredients:

- 1 4 tbsp. almond flour
- 1 tbsp. coconut flour
- 1 tsp. mixed dried herbs (basil, oregano, thyme)
- ½ tsp. organic baking powder
- ½ tsp. garlic powder
- ½ tsp. onion powder
- Salt and ground black pepper, as required
- ¼ C. cream cheese, softened
- 3 large organic eggs
- ½ C. cheddar cheese, grated
- 1/3 C. Parmesan cheese, grated

Instructions:

1) Preheat the waffle iron and then grease it.
2) In a bowl, mix together the flours, dried herbs, baking powder and seasoning and mix well.
3) In another bowl, add the cream cheese and eggs and beat until well combined.
4) Add the flour mixture, cheddar and Parmesan cheese and mix until well combined.
5) Place desired amount of the mixture into preheated waffle iron.
6) Cook for about 2-3 minutes or until desired doneness.
7) Repeat with the remaining mixture.
8) Serve warm.

Nutrition Information:

Calories per serving: 243; Carbohydrates: 5.3g; Protein: 14.1g; Fat: 19.2g; Sugar: 1.1g; Sodium: 288mg; Fiber: 2.1g

Sweet & Zesty Muffin

Serves: 6

Preparation Time: 15 minutes, Cooking Time: 30 minutes

Ingredients:

- ½ C. coconut flour, sifted
- ½ tsp. organic baking soda
- 6 organic eggs
- ½ C. butter, melted
- 1 tbsp. fresh lemon juice
- 1 tsp. fresh lemon zest
- 1 tsp. stevia powder extract
- 1 C. fresh cranberries, minced

Instructions:

1) Preheat the oven to 350 degrees F. Line a 12 cups muffin tin.
2) In a bowl, add the flour and baking soda and mix well.
3) In another bowl, add the remaining ingredients except the cranberries and beat until well combined.
4) Add the flour mixture and mix until just combined.
5) Gently, fold in the cranberries.
6) Transfer the mixture into prepared muffin cups evenly.
7) Bake for about 25-30 minutes or until a toothpick inserted in the center comes out clean.
8) Remove the muffin tin from oven and keep on wire rack to cool for about 10 minutes.
9) Carefully invert the muffins onto a wire rack to cool completely before serving.

Nutrition Information:

Calories per serving: 214; Carbohydrates: 2.8g; Protein: 5.9g; Fat: 19.9g; Sugar: 1.2g; Sodium: 278mg; Fiber: 1.1g

Perfect Broccoli Muffins

Serves: 6

Preparation Time: 15 minutes, Cooking Time: 20 minutes

Ingredients:

- 2 tbsp. unsalted butter
- 6 large organic eggs
- ½ C. heavy whipping cream
- ½ C. Parmesan cheese, grated
- Salt and freshly ground black pepper, to taste
- 1¼ C. broccoli, chopped
- 2 tbsp. fresh parsley, chopped
- ½ C. Swiss cheese, grated

Instructions:

1) Preheat the oven to 350 degrees F. Grease a 12 cups muffin tin.
2) In a bowl, add the eggs, cream, Parmesan cheese, salt and black pepper and beat until well combined.
3) Divide the broccoli and parsley in the bottom of each prepared muffin cups evenly.
4) Top with the egg mixture, followed by the Swiss cheese.
5) Bake for about 20 minutes, rotating the pan once halfway through.
6) Remove from the oven and place onto a wire rack for about 5 minutes before serving.
7) Carefully, invert the muffins onto a serving platter and serve warm.

Nutrition Information:

Calories per serving: 205; Carbohydrates: 2.5g; Protein: 12.2g; Fat: 16.7g; Sugar: 0.9g; Sodium: 210mg; Fiber: 0.5g

Staple Breakfast Bread

Serves: 16

Preparation Time: 20 minutes, Cooking Time: 40 minutes

Ingredients:

- 2 C. almond flour
- 1 tbsp. psyllium husk powder
- 1 tsp. xanthan gum
- 1 tsp. organic baking powder
- Pinch of salt
- 2 tsp. dry yeast
- 1 tsp. inulin
- 2 tbsp. warm water
- 4½ oz. butter, melted
- 7 organic eggs

Instructions:

1) Line a 9x5-inch loaf pan with parchment paper.
2) In a large bowl, add the almond flour, psyllium husk, xanthan gum, baking powder gum and salt and mix well.
3) With your hands, create a well in the center of flour mixture.
4) In the well, add the yeast, inulin and warm water.
5) Carefully, mix the warm water into the yeast and inulin.
6) Set aside for about 10 minutes.
7) Add the butter and eggs and mix until well combined.
8) Place the mixture into the prepared loaf pan evenly.
9) With a tea towel, cover the loaf pan and set aside at a warm place for about 20 minutes.

10) Preheat the oven to 340 degrees F.

11) Remove the tea towel and bake for about 30-40 minutes or until a tooth pick inserted in the center comes out clean.

12) Remove the loaf pan from oven and place on a wire rack to cool for at least 10-15 minutes.

13) Carefully, invert the bread onto rack to cool completely.

14) With a sharp knife, cut the bread loaf in desired size slices and serve.

Nutrition Information:

Calories per serving: 169; Carbohydrates: 4.4g; Protein: 5.7g; Fat: 15.4g; Sugar: 0.7g; Sodium: 89mg; Fiber: 2.4g

Aromatic Cinnamon Bread

Serves: 10

Preparation Time: 15 minutes, Cooking Time: 30 minutes

Ingredients:

- ½ C. coconut flour
- 2 tbsp. granulated Erythritol
- 1/8 tsp. xanthan gum
- ½ tsp. baking soda
- ½ tsp. organic baking powder
- 2 tsp. ground cinnamon
- ½ tsp. ground ginger
- ¼ tsp. ground nutmeg
- ¼ tsp. salt
- 4 large organic eggs
- ½ C. butter
- 1/3 C. unsweetened almond milk
- 1 tsp. organic vanilla extract
- ½ tsp. organic apple cider vinegar
- 1 oz. carrots, peeled and shredded
- 1 oz. pecans, chopped

Instructions:

1) Preheat the oven to 300 degrees F. Grease a 9x5-inch loaf pan.
2) In a bowl, add the coconut flour, Erythritol, xanthan gum, baking soda, baking powder, spices and salt and mix well.
3) Ina another bowl, add the eggs, butter, almond milk, vanilla extract and vinegar and beat until well combined.

4) Add the flour mixture and mix until just combined.

5) Gently, fold in the carrots.

6) Place the mixture into the prepared loaf pan evenly and top sprinkle with the pecans.

7) Bake for about 20-30 minutes or until a tooth pick inserted in the center comes out clean.

8) Remove the loaf pan from oven and place on a wire rack to cool for at least 10-15 minutes.

9) Carefully, invert the bread onto rack to cool completely.

10) With a sharp knife, cut the bread loaf in desired size slices and serve.

Nutrition Information:

Calories per serving: 140; Carbohydrates: 2.3g; Protein: 3.1g; Fat: 13.5g; Sugar: 0.5g; Sodium: 231mg; Fiber: 1.3g

Fluffy Broccoli Omelet

Serves: 8

Preparation Time: 15 minutes, Cooking Time: 41 minutes

Ingredients:

- 20 oz. frozen broccoli florets
- 12 organic eggs
- 1 C. half-and-half
- ¼ tsp. fresh rosemary, minced
- ¼ tsp. ground nutmeg
- ¼ tsp. red pepper flakes, crushed
- Salt and freshly ground black pepper, to taste
- 6 oz. sharp cheddar cheese, grated

Instructions:

1) Preheat the oven to 350 degrees F. Lightly, grease 8 wide mouth mason jars.
2) In a pan of lightly salted boiling water, add the broccoli and cook for about 1 minute.
3) Drain the broccoli well and pat dry with paper towel.
4) Now, chop the broccoli florets roughly.
5) In a large bowl, add the remaining ingredients except cheese and beat until well combined.
6) Add the broccoli and cheese and stir to combine.
7) Arrange the jars into a rimmed baking dish.
8) Bake for about 35-40 minutes.
9) Remove from the oven and serve hot.

Nutrition Information:

Calories per serving: 244; Carbohydrates: 6.9g; Protein: 16.5g; Fat: 17.4g; Sugar: 1.9g; Sodium: 280mg; Fiber: 1.9g

Southwest Tofu Scramble

Serves: 3

Preparation Time: 15 minutes, Cooking Time: 13 minutes

Ingredients:

- 1 tsp. olive oil
- 1 small garlic clove, minced
- 2 small tomatoes, chopped finely
- ¾ C. fresh mushrooms, chopped
- 1 lb. extra-firm tofu, drained, pressed and crumbled
- 1 tsp. freshly squeezed lemon juice
- ½ tsp. low-sodium soy sauce
- Pinch of freshly ground black pepper
- 1 tbsp. fresh parsley leaves, chopped finely

Instructions:

1) In a large nonstick skillet, heat the oil over medium heat and sauté the garlic for about 1 minute.
2) Add the tomatoes and mushrooms and cook for about 3-4 minutes, stirring frequently.
3) Add the tofu, lemon juice, soy sauce and black pepper and cook for about 6-8 minutes, stirring frequently.
4) Remove from the heat and serve hot with the garnishing of parsley.

Nutrition Information:

Calories per serving: 168; Carbohydrates: 6.5g; Protein: 16.2g; Fat: 10.6g; Sugar: 2.8g; Sodium: 66mg; Fiber: 1.6g

Stuffed Avocado Cups

Serves: 4

Preparation Time: 15 minutes, Cooking Time: 15 minutes

Ingredients:

- 2 ripe avocados, halved lengthwise and pitted
- ½ tsp. garlic powder
- 4 medium organic eggs
- Salt and freshly ground black pepper, to taste
- 2 tbsp. Parmesan cheese, shredded
- 1 tsp. fresh chives, minced

Instructions:

1) Preheat oven to 350 degrees F. Line a baking sheet with a piece of foil.
2) Carefully, scoop out 1-2 tbsp. of flesh from the center of each avocado half.
3) Arrange avocado halves onto the prepared baking sheet, cut side up.
4) Sprinkle each avocado half evenly with garlic powder.
5) Carefully, crack one egg into each avocado half.
6) Sprinkle each egg with salt and black pepper and then, top evenly with the cheese.
7) Bake for about 12-15 minutes or until desired doneness of the egg whites.
8) Garnish with fresh chives and serve warm.

Nutrition Information:

Calories per serving: 280; Carbohydrates: 9.2g; Protein: 8.5g; Fat: 24.7g; Sugar: 0.9g; Sodium: 149mg; Fiber: 6.8g

Classic Sausage Frittata

Serves: 8

Preparation Time: 15 minutes, Cooking Time: 50 minutes

Ingredients:

- 12 oz. mild sausage, crumbled
- ½ C. feta cheese, crumbled
- 12 organic eggs
- ½ C. unsweetened almond milk
- ½ C. heavy cream
- ¼ tsp. ground nutmeg
- Salt and freshly ground black pepper, to taste
- 10 oz. pack frozen chopped spinach, thawed, squeezed   and torn

Instructions:

1) Preheat oven to 375 degrees F. Lightly, grease a 13x9 casserole dish.
2) In a large bowl, add the eggs, almond milk, s cream, nutmeg, salt and black pepper and beat until well combined.
3) In another large bowl, add the sausage, spinach and feta cheese and gently, toss to coat.
4) Place the sausage mixture into the bottom of the prepared casserole dish evenly and top with the egg mixture.
5) Bake for about 50 minutes or until top becomes golden brown.
6) Remove from oven and place onto a wire rack for about 5 minutes before slicing.
7) Cut into desired sized wedges and serve.

Nutrition Information:

Calories per serving: 131; Carbohydrates: 2.2g; Protein: 9.5g; Fat: 9.7g; Sugar: 0.7g; Sodium: 282mg; Fiber: 0.9g

Crustless Quiche

Serves: 6

Cooking Time: 40 minutes, Preparation Time: 15 minutes

Ingredients:

- 1/3 lb. cooked bacon, chopped
- 1 (16-oz.) bag frozen spinach, thawed and squeezed
- ¼ of medium onion, minced
- 6 large organic eggs
- 8 oz. Swiss cheese, grated
- ¾ C. heavy cream
- 1 tsp. fresh lemon zest, grated
- Salt and freshly ground black pepper, to taste

Instructions:

1) Preheat oven to 350 degrees F. Arrange a rack into the middle of the oven.
2) Grease an 8x8-inch glass baking dish.
3) In a large bowl, add all the ingredients and with a hand mixer, mix until well combined.
4) Place the mixture into the prepared baking dish evenly.
8) Bake for about 40 minutes or until top becomes golden brown.
9) Remove from oven and place onto a wire rack for about 5 minutes before slicing.
10) Cut into desired sized wedges and serve.

Nutrition Information:

Calories per serving: 352; Carbohydrates: 6.1g; Protein: 22.1g; Fat: 26.9g; Sugar: 1.1g; Sodium: 1011mg; Fiber: 1.8g

Mediterranean Breakfast

Serves: 4

Cooking Time: 20 minutes, Preparation Time: 15 minutes

Ingredients:
- 2 tbsp. butter
- 1/3 C. scallion, chopped
- 10 C. fresh baby spinach, chopped
- ¼ tsp. red pepper flakes, crushed
- Salt and freshly ground black pepper, to taste
- 4 organic egg
- 2 tbsp. mozzarella cheese, shredded
- 1 tbsp. fresh parsley, chopped

Instructions:
1) Preheat the oven to 400 degrees F.
2) In an ovenproof skillet, melt the butter over medium heat and cook the scallion for about 2 minutes.
3) Add the spinach, red pepper flakes, salt and black pepper and cook for about 2-3 minutes or until wilted, stirring frequently.
4) Remove from the heat and discard any extra liquid from the skillet.
5) Make 4 wells in the spinach mixture.
6) Carefully crack 1 egg in each well.
7) Bake for about 10-15 minutes or until the organic egg whites are set.
8) Top with mozzarella cheese and parsley and serve.

Nutrition Information:
Calories per serving: 174; Carbohydrates: 4.3g; Protein: 11.9g; Fat: 13g; Sugar: 0.9g; Sodium: 287mg; Fiber: 1.9g

Chapter 3 Lunch Recipes

Marinated Tomato Salad

Serves: 4

Preparation Time: 15 minutes

Ingredients:

For Marinade:

- 1 garlic clove, minced finely
- ¼ C. olive oil
- 1 tbsp. prepared pesto
- 3 tbsp. balsamic vinegar
- ¼ tsp. Erythritol
- Salt and freshly ground black pepper, to taste

For Salad:

- 2 C. yellow grape tomatoes, halved
- 2 C. red grape tomatoes, halved
- ½ of red onion, sliced thinly
- 3 tbsp. fresh parsley, minced
- 1 head iceberg lettuce, torn

Instructions:

1) For marinade: in a large bowl, add all the ingredients and mix until well combined.
2) Add the tomatoes, onion and parsley and mix until well combined.
3) Cover the bowl and refrigerate for about 4-6 hours.
4) Before serving, in a large serving bowl, place the lettuce and tomato mixture and toss to coat well.
5) Serve immediately.

Nutrition Information:

Calories per serving: 143; Carbohydrates: 9g; Protein: 2.1g; Fat: 11.8g; Sugar: 5g; Sodium: 63mg; Fiber: 2.5g

Crunchy Lunch Salad

Serves: 2

Preparation Time: 20 minutes

Ingredients:

For Dressing:

- 1 garlic clove, minced
- 2/3 C. plain Greek yogurt
- ½ tbsp. Dijon mustard
- Salt and freshly ground black pepper, to taste

For Salad:

- 2 medium cucumbers, spiralized with Blade C
- 2 large hard-boiled eggs, peeled and chopped
- ½ C. celery, chopped
- 2 tbsp. walnuts, toasted and chopped

Instructions:

1) For dressing: in a bowl, add all the ingredients and beat until well combined.
2) In a large serving bowl, mix together the cucumber, eggs and celery.
3) Pour the dressing over salad and toss to coat well.
4) Top with walnuts and serve.

Nutrition Information:

Calories per serving: 195; Carbohydrates: 10g; Protein: 13.7g; Fat: 10.9g; Sugar: 4g; Sodium: 838mg; Fiber: 1.8g

Fabulous Salmon Salad

Serves: 4

Preparation Time: 15 minutes

Ingredients:

For Salad:

- 1 lb. fresh asparagus, trimmed and cut into 1-inch pieces
- ½ lb. smoked salmon, cut into bite sized pieces
- 2 heads red leaf lettuce, torn
- ½ C. pecans, toasted and chopped

For Dressing:

- 2 tbsp. fresh lemon juice
- ¼ C. olive oil
- 1 tsp. Dijon mustard
- Salt and freshly ground black pepper, to taste

Instructions:

1) In a pan of the boiling water, add the asparagus and cook for about 5 minutes.
2) Drain the asparagus well.
3) In a large bowl, add the asparagus and remaining salad ingredients and mix.
4) For dressing: in another bowl, add all the ingredients and beat until well combined.
5) Pour the dressing over salad and gently, toss to coat well.
6) Serve immediately.

Nutrition Information:

Calories per serving: 279; Carbohydrates: 10g; Protein: 14.6g; Fat: 21.5g; Sugar: 4.2g; Sodium: 1000mg; Fiber: 4.4g

Creamy Shrimp Salad

Serves: 12

Cooking Time: 3 minutes, Preparation Time: 20 minutes

Ingredients:

- 4 lb. large shrimp
- 1 lemon, quartered
- 3 C. celery stalks, chopped
- 1 yellow onion, chopped
- 2 C. mayonnaise
- 2 tbsp. fresh lemon juice
- 1 tsp. Dijon mustard
- Salt and freshly ground black pepper, to taste

Instructions:

1) In a pan of the lightly salted boiling water, add the shrimp, and lemon and cook for about 3 minutes.
2) Drain the shrimps well and let them cool.
3) Then, peel and devein the shrimps.
4) In a large bowl, add the cooked shrimp and remaining ingredients and gently, stir to combine.
5) Serve immediately.

Nutrition Information:

Calories per serving: 429; Carbohydrates: 4.1g; Protein: 34.8g; Fat: 29.3g; Sugar: 0.8g; Sodium: 648mg; Fiber: 0.7g

Dairy-Free Creamy Soup

Serves: 6

Preparation Time: 15 minutes

Ingredients:

- 3 large avocados, peeled, pitted and roughly chopped
- 1/3 C. fresh cilantro leaves
- 3 C. homemade vegetable broth
- 2 tbsp. fresh lemon juice
- 1 tsp. ground cumin
- ¼ tsp. cayenne pepper
- Salt, to taste

Instructions:

1) In a high-speed blender, add all the ingredients and pulse on high speed until smooth.
2) Transfer the soup into a large serving bowl.
3) Cover the bowl and refrigerate to chill for at least 2-3 hours.
4) Serve chilled.

Nutrition Information:

Calories per serving: 227; Carbohydrates: 9.4g; Protein: 4.5g; Fat: 20.4g; Sugar: 1g; Sodium: 417mg; Fiber: 6.8g

Vibrant Tomato Soup

Serves: 8

Cooking Time: 28 minutes, Preparation Time: 15 minutes

Ingredients:

- 3 tbsp. olive oil
- 2 small yellow onions, thinly sliced
- Salt, to taste
- 3 tsp. curry powder
- 1 tsp. ground cumin
- 1 tsp. ground coriander
- ½ tsp. red pepper flakes, crushed

- 1 (14-oz.) can sugar-free diced tomatoes with juice
- 1 (28-oz.) can sugar-free plum tomatoes with juices
- 5½ C. homemade vegetable broth
- ¼ C. fresh basil leaves, chopped

Instructions:

1) In a large Dutch oven, heat the oil over medium-low heat and cook the onion with 1 tsp. of the salt for about 10-12 minutes, stirring occasionally.
2) Stir in the spices and sauté for about 1 minute.
3) Add the both cans of tomatoes alongside the juices and broth and stir to combine.
4) Increase the heat to medium-high and cook until boiling.
5) Reduce the heat to medium-low and simmer for about 15 minutes.
6) Remove from the heat and with a hand blender, blend the soup until smooth.
7) Top with the fresh basil and serve.

Nutrition Information:

Calories per serving: 113; Carbohydrates: 9.4g; Protein: 5.1g; Fat: 2.7g; Sugar: 5g; Sodium: 553mg; Fiber: 6.7g

Rich Cauliflower Soup

Serves: 5

Cooking Time: 25 minutes, Preparation Time: 15 minutes

Ingredients:

- 2 tbsp. olive oil
- 1 small yellow onion, chopped
- 2 small carrots, peeled and chopped
- 2 small celery stalks, chopped
- 2 garlic cloves, minced
- 1 Serrano pepper, finely chopped
- 1 tsp. ground turmeric
- 1 tsp. ground coriander
- 1 tsp. ground cumin
- ¼ tsp. red pepper flakes, crushed
- 1 head cauliflower, chopped
- 4 C. homemade vegetable broth
- 1 C. unsweetened coconut milk
- 2 tbsp. freshly squeezed lime juice
- Salt and freshly ground black pepper, to taste
- 2 tbsp. fresh cilantro, finely chopped
- 1 tsp. fresh lime zest, grated finely

Instructions:

1) In a large soup pan, heat the oil over medium heat and sauté the onion, carrot and celery for about 4 minutes.
2) Add the garlic, Serrano pepper and spices and sauté for about 1 minute.
3) Add the cauliflower and cook for about 5 minutes, stirring occasionally.
4) Add the broth and coconut milk and stir to combine.
5) Increase the heat to medium-high and bring to a boil.
6) Reduce the heat to low and simmer, partially covered for about 15 minutes.
7) Stir in the lime juice, salt, and black pepper and remove from the heat.
8) Serve hot with the topping of cilantro and lime zest.

Nutrition Information:

Calories per serving: 121; Carbohydrates: 8.3g; Protein: 5.5g; Fat: 7.7g; Sugar: 3.6g; Sodium: 676mg; Fiber: 2.7g

Crunchy Chicken Salad Wraps

Serves: 4

Preparation Time: 15 minutes

Ingredients:

- 1½ lb. grass-fed cooked chicken, cubed
- 1 C. fresh cranberries
- 1 C. celery, chopped
- ½ C. plain Greek yogurt
- ½ C. pecans, chopped
- ½ C. mayonnaise
- ½ tsp. Dijon mustard
- Salt and freshly ground black pepper, to taste
- 12 large bib lettuce leaves, rinsed and pat dried

Instructions:

1) In a large bowl, add all the ingredients except the lettuce and gently, stir to combine.
2) Arrange the lettuce leaves onto a smooth surface.
3) Divide the chicken mixture onto each lettuce leaf evenly.
4) Top with the Parmesan and chives and serve immediately.

Nutrition Information:

Calories per serving: 392; Carbohydrates: 5.4g; Protein: 35.3g; Fat: 24.5g; Sugar: 2.8g; Sodium: 252mg; Fiber: 2.1g

Thai Salad Wraps

Serves: 6

Cooking Time: 20 minutes, Preparation Time: 20 minutes

Ingredients:

- 2 tbsp. unsalted butter
- 1 lb. grass-fed lean ground beef
- 1 yellow onion, chopped
- 2 garlic cloves, minced
- 1 bell pepper, seeded and chopped
- 1 C. carrot, peeled and chopped
- ½ C. yellow squash, chopped
- ½ C. zucchini, chopped
- 2 tbsp. low-sodium soy sauce
- ½ tsp. curry powder
- Freshly ground black pepper, to taste
- 12 lettuce leaves
- 1½ C. Parmesan cheese, shredded

Instructions:

1) In a large skillet, melt the butter over medium heat and cook the beef for about 8-10 minutes, breaking the lumps.
2) Stir in the vegetables and cook for about 4-5 minutes.
3) Stir in the soy sauce, curry powder and black pepper and cook for about 4-5 minutes.
4) Remove from the heat and set aside to cool slightly.
5) Arrange lettuce leaves onto serving plates and top each with beef mixture evenly.
6) Sprinkle with cheese and serve.

Nutrition Information:

Calories per serving: 280; Carbohydrates: 7.4g; Protein: 24.2g; Fat: 16.1g; Sugar: 3.5g; Sodium: 726mg; Fiber: 1.5g

Thanksgiving Favorite Burgers

Serves: 4

Cooking Time: 10 minutes, Preparation Time: 15 minutes

Ingredients:

- 1 lb. ground turkey
- 10 oz. feta cheese, crumbled
- 1 organic egg, beaten
- 10 oz. black olives, pitted and chopped
- 1 tsp. garlic powder
- Salt and freshly ground black pepper, to taste
- 1 tbsp. unsalted butter
- 6 C. fresh baby spinach

Instructions:

1) In a bowl, add the turkey, cheese, egg, olives, garlic powder, salt, and black pepper and mix well.
2) Make 4 equal-sized patties from the mixture.
3) Arrange the patties onto a parchment paper lined baking sheet and refrigerate for about 15 minutes.
4) In a skillet, melt the butter over medium heat and cook the patties for about 3-5 minutes or until desired doneness.
5) Divide the spinach onto serving plates.
6) Top each plate with 1 patty and serve.

Nutrition Information:

Calories per serving: 544; Carbohydrates: 9.4g; Protein: 39.3g; Fat: 44.5g; Sugar: 3.3g; Sodium: 900mg; Fiber: 3.4g

Juiciest Beef Burgers

Serves: 4

Cooking Time: 12 minutes, Preparation Time: 15 minutes

Ingredients:

- 1½ lb. grass-fed ground chuck
- Salt and freshly ground black pepper, to taste
- 2 C. fresh spinach
- ½ C. mozzarella cheese, shredded
- 2 tbsp. Parmesan cheese, grated

Instructions:

1) In a bowl, add the beef, salt and black pepper and mix until well combined.
2) Make 8 equal sized patties from the mixture.
3) Arrange the patties onto a plate and refrigerate until using.
4) In a frying pan, add the spinach over medium-high heat and cook, covered for about 2 minutes or until wilted.
5) Drain the spinach and set aside to cool.
6) With your hands squeeze the spinach to extract the liquid completely.
7) Place the spinach onto a cutting board and then, chop it.
8) In a bowl, add the chopped spinach and both cheese and mix well.
9) Place about ¼ C. of the spinach mixture in the center of 4 patties and top each with the remaining 4 patties.
10) With your fingers, press the edges firmly to seal the filling.
11) Then, press each patty slightly to flatten.
12) Heat a lightly, greased grill pan over medium-high heat and cook the patties for about 5-6 minutes per side.
13) Serve hot.

Nutrition Information:

Calories per serving: 338; Carbohydrates: 0.7g; Protein: 54g; Fat: 11.9g; Sugar: 0.1g; Sodium: 205mg; Fiber: 0.3g

Pool-Side Lunch Burgers

Serves: 4

Cooking Time: 8 minutes, Preparation Time: 15 minutes

Ingredients:

- 1 lb. grass-fed ground lamb
- ¼ yellow onion, chopped
- 2 garlic cloves, minced
- 2 tsp. fresh oregano, minced
- 1 tsp. fresh lemon zest, finely grated
- Salt and freshly ground black pepper, to taste
- 6 C. lettuce, torn

Instructions:

1) Preheat the grill to medium-high heat. Grease the grill grate.
2) In a bowl, add the lamb, onion, garlic, oregano, lemon zest, salt, and black pepper and with your hands, mix until well combined.
3) Make 8 small equal-sized patties from the mixture.
4) Grill the patties for about 4 minutes per side or until desired doneness.
5) Divide the lettuces onto serving plates.
6) Top each with 2 burgers and serve.

Nutrition Information:

Calories per serving: 230; Carbohydrates: 4.4g; Protein: 32.5g; Fat: 8.6g; Sugar: 1.2g; Sodium: 325mg; Fiber: 1.1g

Savory Zucchini Cake

Serves: 8
Cooking Time: 52 minutes, Preparation Time: 15 minutes

Ingredients:

- 2 tbsp. olive oil
- 1 large zucchini, grated
- 6 large organic eggs (whites and yolks separated)
- 2 scallions, chopped
- 2 tbsp. fresh mint leaves, chopped
- ½ C. Parmesan cheese, grated
- ½ C. feta cheese, crumbled
- ½ C. coconut flour
- ½ tsp. organic baking powder
- 1 tsp. garlic powder
- Salt and freshly ground black pepper, to taste

Instructions:

1) Preheat the oven to 400 degrees F. Line the bottom of a greased springform pan with parchment paper.
2) In a frying pan, heat oil over medium heat and cook the zucchini for about 10-12 minutes, stirring occasionally.
3) Remove from the heat and set aside to cool slightly.
4) Meanwhile, in a bowl, add the egg whites and beat until stiff peaks form.
5) In another bowl, add the zucchini, egg yolks and the remaining ingredients and mix until well combined.
6) Gently fold in the whipped egg whites.
7) Place the mixture into the prepared pan evenly.
8) Bake for about 40 minutes.
9) Remove from the oven and set aside to cool for about 10 minutes before serving.
10) Cut into 8 equal sized wedges and serve.

Nutrition Information:

Calories per serving: 140; Carbohydrates: 3.3g; Protein: 8.9g; Fat: 10.7g; Sugar: 1.6g; Sodium: 227mg; Fiber: 1g

Refreshingly Tasty Meatballs

Serves: 6

Cooking Time: 18 minutes, Preparation Time: 15 minutes

Ingredients:

For Meatballs:

- 1 lb. grass-fed lean ground chicken
- 2 oz. cheddar cheese, grated
- 2 tbsp. almond flour
- 2 tbsp. golden flax meal
- ½ of medium red bell pepper, seeded and chopped
- 2 medium scallions, chopped
- 2 tbsp. fresh cilantro, chopped
- 1 tsp. fresh lime zest, grated finely
- 1 tbsp. fresh lime juice
- ½ tsp. garlic powder
- ½ tsp. red pepper flakes, crushed

For Guacamole:

- 1 large avocado, peeled, pitted and chopped
- 1 tbsp. fresh lime juice
- ¼ tsp. garlic powder
- Salt and freshly ground black pepper, to taste

Instructions:

1) Preheat the oven to 350 degrees F. Grease a large baking sheet.
2) For meatballs: in a bowl, add all the ingredients and mix until well combined.
3) Make equal sized meatballs from chicken mixture.
4) Arrange balls onto prepared baking sheet and bake for about 15-18 minutes.
5) Meanwhile, for guacamole: in a bowl, add all ingredients and with a fork, mash until well combined.
6) Serve meatballs alongside the guacamole.

Nutrition Information:

Calories per serving: 236; Carbohydrates: 5.5g; Protein: 19.6g; Fat: 15.7g; Sugar: 1g; Sodium: 172mg; Fiber: 3.2g

Flavor Packed Meatballs

Serves: 6

Cooking Time: 1 hour 10 minutes, Preparation Time: 15 minutes

Ingredients:

For Meatballs:

- 1 lb. grass-fed ground beef
- 1 tbsp. olive oil
- 1 tsp. dehydrated onion flakes, crushed
- ½ tsp. granulated garlic
- ½ tsp. ground cumin
- ½ tsp. red pepper flakes, crushed
- Salt, to taste

For Tomato Chutney:

- 2 C. green tomatoes, chopped
- 2 tbsp. fresh red chili, chopped
- 1 tbsp. fresh ginger, peeled and chopped
- ½ tbsp. fresh lime zest, grated
- ¼ C. organic apple cider vinegar
- 2 tbsp. red boat fish sauce
- 1 tbsp. fresh lime juice
- 2 tbsp. Erythritol
- ¼ tsp. mustard powder
- ½ tsp. dried onion flakes
- ½ tsp. ground coriander
- ½ tsp. ground cinnamon
- ¼ tsp. ground allspice
- 1/8 tsp. ground cloves

- Salt, to taste
- 2 tbsp. fresh cilantro, chopped

Instructions:

1) For chutney: add all the ingredient in a pan over medium heat except for cilantro and bring to a boil.
2) Reduce the heat to low and simmer for about 45 minutes, stirring occasionally.
3) Remove from heat and set aside to cool.
4) After cooling, stir in the fresh cilantro.
5) Meanwhile, preheat the oven to 400 degrees F. Line a large baking sheet with parchment paper.
6) For meatballs: in a large mixing bowl, add all the ingredients and with your hands, mix until well combined.
7) Shape the mixture into desired and equal-sized balls.
8) Arrange meatballs into the prepared baking sheet in a single layer.
9) Bake for about 15-20 minutes or until done completely.
10) Serve the meatballs with chutney.

Nutrition Information:

Calories per serving: 183; Carbohydrates: 4.6g; Protein: 24.1g; Fat: 7.4g; Sugar: 2.3g; Sodium: 545mg; Fiber: 1.3g

Appealing Zucchini Boats

Serves: 3

Cooking Time: 20 minutes, Preparation Time: 20 minutes

Ingredients:

- 3 medium zucchinis, halved lengthwise
- 3 tbsp. olive oil, divided
- ¾ lb. grass-fed chicken breast, cut into cubes
- ¼ tsp. Italian seasoning
- ¼ tsp. garlic powder
- Salt and freshly ground black pepper, to taste
- ¾ C. sugar-free pasta sauce
- ¼ C. Parmesan cheese, grated
- ¼ C. mozzarella cheese, shredded
- 2 tbsp. fresh parsley, chopped finely

Instructions:

1) Preheat the oven to 400 degrees F. Grease a large baking sheet.
2) With a melon baller, scoop out the flesh of each zucchini half. Discard the flesh.
3) Coat the zucchini halves with 2 tbsp. of the oil.
4) Arrange the zucchini halves into a baking dish, cut-side up.
5) Bake for about 15 minutes or until the zucchini becomes tender.
6) Meanwhile, in a large non-stick skillet, heat the remaining olive oil over medium-high heat and cook the chicken along with the Italian seasoning, salt and black pepper for about 8-10 minutes or until the chicken is cooked through, stirring occasionally.
7) Stir in the pasta sauce and cook for about 2 minutes, stirring occasionally.

8) Remove from the heat and set aside.

9) Remove the baking dish from the oven and stuff each zucchini half with the chicken mixture evenly.

10) Top each zucchini half with the Parmesan and mozzarella cheese.

11) Bake for about 5 minutes.

12) Garnish with parsley and serve hot.

Nutrition Information:

Calories per serving: 390; Carbohydrates: 10g; Protein: 32.5g; Fat: 25.3g; Sugar: 5g; Sodium: 445mg; Fiber: 2.9g

Unstuffed Cabbage Casserole

Serves: 3

Cooking Time: 30 minutes, Preparation Time: 15 minutes

Ingredients:

- ½ head green cabbage
- 2 scallions, chopped
- 4 tbsp. unsalted butter
- 2 oz. cream cheese, softened
- ¼ C. Parmesan cheese, grated
- ¼ C. cream
- ½ tsp. Dijon mustard
- 2 tbsp. fresh parsley, chopped
- Salt and freshly ground black pepper, to taste

Instructions:

1) Preheat the oven to 350 degrees F.
2) Cut cabbage head in half, lengthwise and then cut into 4 equal sized wedges.
3) In a pan of boiling water, add cabbage wedges and simmer, covered for about 5 minutes.
4) Drain well and arrange cabbage wedges in a small baking dish.
5) In a small pan, melt butter and sauté onions for about 5 minutes.
6) Add the remaining ingredients and stir to combine.
7) Remove from the heat and immediately, place the cheese mixture over cabbage wedges evenly.
8) Bake for about 20 minutes.
9) Remove from the oven and set aside to cool for about 5 minutes before serving.
10) Cut into 3 equal sized portions and serve.

Nutrition Information:

Calories per serving: 273; Carbohydrates: 9g; Protein: 6.2g; Fat: 15.4g; Sugar: 4g; Sodium: 313mg; Fiber: 3.4g

Brilliant Cheesy Broccoli

Serves: 4

Cooking Time: 24 minutes, Preparation Time: 15 minutes

Ingredients:

- 1 lb. fresh broccoli florets
- 3½ oz. butter, melted
- Salt and freshly ground black pepper, to taste
- 5 oz. cheddar cheese, shredded

Instructions:

1) Preheat the oven to 400 degrees F. Generously, grease a baking dish.
2) Ina pan of the lightly salted boiling water, cook the broccoli for bout 3-4 minutes.
3) Drain the broccoli well and transfer into a bowl.
4) Add the butter, salt and black pepper and toss to coat well.
5) Arrange the broccoli florets into the prepared baking dish in a single layer and sprinkle with the cheese.
6) Bake for about 15-20 minutes or until the top becomes brown.
7) Serve hot.

Nutrition Information:

Calories per serving: 359; Carbohydrates: 8g; Protein: 12.2g; Fat: 32.2g; Sugar: 2.1g; Sodium: 430mg; Fiber: 3g

High Protein Lunch

Serves: 3

Cooking Time: 15 minutes, Preparation Time: 15 minutes

Ingredients:
- 2 tbsp. olive oil
- 1 small yellow onion, chopped
- 2 small garlic cloves, minced
- ½ tsp. fresh ginger, minced
- 2 tsp. fresh basil, chopped
- ½ tsp. red pepper flakes, crushed
- ½ lb. firm tofu, drained, pressed and cubed
- 4 C. fresh spinach, chopped
- Salt and freshly ground black pepper, to taste
- 1 tbsp. fresh lemon juice
- 1 tsp. white sesame seeds, toasted

Instructions:
1) In a medium nonstick skillet, heat the oil over medium heat and sauté the onion for about 3-4 minutes.
2) Stir in the garlic, ginger, basil and red pepper flakes and sauté for about 1 minute.
3) Add the tofu cubes and stir fry for about 5-6 minutes.
4) Add the spinach, salt and black pepper and stir fry for about 3-4 minutes.
5) Stir in the lemon juice and remove from the heat.
6) Serve hot with the garnishing of the sesame seeds.

Nutrition Information:
Calories per serving: 162; Carbohydrates: 6.2g; Protein: 8g; Fat: 13.1g; Sugar: 1.8g; Sodium: 94mg; Fiber: 2.3g

Timeless Luncheon Scallops

Serves: 3

Cooking Time: 5 minutes, Preparation Time: 15 minutes

Ingredients:

- ¼ C. unsalted butter
- 2 tbsp. fresh rosemary, chopped
- 2 garlic cloves, minced
- 1 lb. fresh scallops, side muscles removed
- Salt and freshly ground black pepper, to taste

Instructions:

1) In a medium skillet, melt butter over medium-high heat and sauté the rosemary and garlic for about 1 minute.
2) Add the scallops and cook for about 2 minutes per side or until desired doneness.
3) Stir in the salt and black pepper and serve hot.

Nutrition Information:

Calories per serving: 362; Carbohydrates: 2.1g; Protein: 40g; Fat: 17.5g; Sugar: 0g; Sodium: 575mg; Fiber: 1g

Gourmet Shrimp Tacos

Serves: 4

Cooking Time: 15 minutes, Preparation Time: 20 minutes

Ingredients:

For Taco shells:

- 8 oz. cheddar cheese, shredded
- ½ tsp. ground cumin

For Filling:

- 10 oz. shrimp, peeled and deveined
- 2 tbsp. coconut oil
- 2 garlic cloves, chopped finely
- 1 Serrano pepper, seeded and finely chopped
- 1 cup mayonnaise
- 1 tbsp. fresh lime juice
- 1 avocado, peeled, pitted and chopped
- 1 tomato, chopped finely
- 4 tbsp. fresh cilantro, chopped
- Salt and freshly ground black pepper, to taste

Instructions:

1) Preheat the oven to 400 degrees F. Line a baking sheet with parchment paper.
2) For taco shells: in a bowl, add the cheddar cheese and cumin and mix well.
3) Divide the cheese mixture into 6 equal sized portions.
4) Arrange the cheese portions onto the prepared baking sheet in a circle, leaving space between each.

5) Bake for about 10-15 minutes or until the cheese is bubbling and golden brown.

6) Remove from the oven and place the cheese rounds onto a rack to cool for about 30 seconds.

7) Meanwhile, for filling: in a skillet, melt the coconut oil over medium heat and sauté the shrimp with the garlic and Serrano pepper for about 3-4 minutes or until the shrimp are cooked through.

8) Stir in the salt and black pepper and remove from the heat.

9) Set aside to cool.

10) In a large bowl, add the shrimp and remaining ingredients and stir to combine.

11) Place the shrimp mixture into each cheese shell evenly and serve immediately.

Nutrition Information:

Calories per serving: 841; Carbohydrates: 7.5g; Protein: 31.6g; Fat: 76.7g; Sugar: 1.1g; Sodium: 929mg; Fiber: 3.7g

Chapter 4 Dinner Recipes

Filling Shrimp Salad

Serves: 5

Cooking Time: 8 minutes, Preparation Time: 20 minutes

Ingredients:

For Shrimp:

- 2 tbsp. olive oil
- 2 tbsp. fresh key lime juice
- 4 large garlic cloves, peeled
- 2 sprigs fresh rosemary leaves
- ½ tsp. garlic salt
- 20 large shrimp, peeled and deveined

For Salad:

- 1 lb. fresh green beans, trimmed
- ¼ C. olive oil
- 1 onion, sliced
- Salt and freshly ground black pepper, to taste
- ½ C. garlic and herb feta cheese, crumbled

Instructions:

1) For shrimp marinade: in a blender, add all the ingredients except shrimp and pulse until smooth.
2) Transfer the marinade in a large bowl.
3) Add the shrimp and coat with marinade generously.
4) Cover the bowl and refrigerate to marinate for at least 30 minutes.

5) Preheat the broiler of oven. Arrange the rack in top position of the oven. Line a large baking sheet with a piece of foil.

6) Place the shrimp with marinade onto the prepared baking sheet.

7) Broil for about 3-4 minutes per side.

8) Transfer the shrimp mixture into a bowl and refrigerate until using.

9) Meanwhile, for salad: in a pan of the salted boiling water, add the green beans and cook for about 3-4 minutes.

10) Drain the green beans well and rinse under cold running water.

11) Transfer the green beans into a large bowl.

12) Add the onion, shrimp, salt and black pepper and stir to combine.

13) Cover and refrigerate to chill for about 1 hour.

14) Stir in the cheese just before serving.

Nutrition Information:

Calories per serving: 303; Carbohydrates: 10.5g; Protein: 24.3g; Fat: 18.5g; Sugar: 2.5g; Sodium: 420mg; Fiber: 4g

Ultimate Steak Salad

Serves: 5

Cooking Time: 8 minutes, Preparation Time: 20 minutes

Ingredients:

For Steak:

- 1½ lb. grass-fed skirt steak, cut into 4 pieces
- Salt and freshly ground black pepper, to taste

For Salad:

- 2 medium green bell pepper, seeded and sliced thinly
- 2 large tomatoes, sliced
- 1 C. onion, sliced thinly
- 8 C. mixed fresh baby greens
- 1/3 C. feta cheese, crumbled

For Dressing:

- 2 tsp. Dijon mustard
- 4 tbsp. balsamic vinegar
- ½ C. olive oil
- Salt and freshly ground black pepper, to taste

Instructions:

1) Preheat the grill to medium-high heat. Grease the grill grate.
2) Sprinkle the beef steak with salt and black pepper generously.
3) Cover and grill, the steak for 3-4 minutes per side.
4) Transfer the steak onto a cutting board for about 10 minutes before slicing.
5) With a sharp knife, cut the beef steaks into thin slices.
6) Meanwhile, in a large bowl, mix together all salad ingredients.

7) For dressing: in another bowl, add all the ingredients and beat until well combined.

8) Pour the dressing over salad and gently toss to coat well.

9) Divide the salad onto serving plates evenly.

10) Top each plate with a steak slices and serve.

Nutrition Information:

Calories per serving: 521; Carbohydrates: 9g; Protein: 39.5g; Fat: 36.3g; Sugar: 5g; Sodium: 279mg; Fiber: 2.4g

Easy-Going Pork Salad

Serves: 5

Cooking Time: 6 minutes, Preparation Time: 15 minutes

Ingredients:

- 1½ lb. pork tenderloin, sliced thinly
- Salt and freshly ground black pepper, to taste
- 3 tbsp. olive oil
- 2 carrots, peeled and grated
- 5 C. Napa cabbage, shredded
- 2 scallions, chopped
- 2 tsp. red boat fish sauce
- 2 tbsp. fresh lime juice
- ¼ C. fresh mint leaves, chopped

Instructions:

1) Season the pork with salt and black pepper evenly.
2) In a large skillet, heat the oil over medium heat and cook the pork slices for about 2-3 minutes per sides or until cooked through.
3) In a large bowl, add the pork and remaining ingredients except mint leaves and toss to coat well.
4) Serve with the garnishing of mint leaves.

Nutrition Information:

Calories per serving: 292; Carbohydrates: 4.8g; Protein: 37.7g; Fat: 13.4g; Sugar: 2.24g; Sodium: 372mg; Fiber: 1.8g

Mexican Chicken Soup

Serves: 4

Cooking Time: 10 minutes, Preparation Time: 15 minutes

Ingredients:

- ½ C. salsa verde
- 1 C. sharp cheddar cheese
- 4 oz. cream cheese, softened
- 2 C. homemade chicken broth
- 2 C. cooked grass-fed chicken, chopped

Instructions:

1) In a blender, add the salsa, cheddar cheese, cream cheese, and broth and pulse until smooth.
2) Transfer the mixture into a medium-sized pan over medium heat and cook for about 3-5 minutes or until heated through, stirring continuously.
3) Add the chicken and cook for about 3-5 minutes or until heated through, stirring frequently.
4) Serve warm.

Nutrition Information:

Calories per serving: 345; Carbohydrates: 2.9g; Protein: 32.2g; Fat: 22.1g; Sugar: 1g; Sodium: 857mg; Fiber: 0.1g

Beef Taco Soup

Serves: 8

Cooking Time: 27 minutes, Preparation Time: 15 minutes

Ingredients:

- 1 lb. grass-fed ground beef
- ½ C. yellow onion, chopped
- 2 garlic cloves, minced
- 1 tbsp. ground cumin
- 1 tsp. red chili powder
- 8 oz. cream cheese, softened
- 2 (10-oz.) cans sugar-free diced tomatoes with green chiles
- 7¼ C. homemade beef broth
- ½ C. heavy cream
- Salt, as required
- ½ C. fresh cilantro, chopped

Instructions:

1) Heat a large pan over medium-high heat and cook the ground beef, onion, and garlic for about 8-10 minutes, stirring frequently.
2) Drain the grease from pan.
3) In the pan, add the cumin, and chili powder and cook for about 2 minutes.
4) Stir in the cream cheese and cook for about 3-5 minutes, stirring continuously.
5) Stir in the tomatoes, broth, heavy cream, and salt and cook for about 10 minutes.
6) Garnish with cilantro and serve hot.

Nutrition Information:

Calories per serving: 281; Carbohydrates: 6g; Protein: 19.2g; Fat: 19.8g; Sugar: 2.9g; Sodium: 844mg; Fiber: 1.3g

Omega-3 Rich Soup

Serves: 4

Cooking Time: 20 minutes, Preparation Time: 15 minutes

Ingredients:

- 1 tbsp. olive oil
- 1 yellow onion, chopped
- 1 garlic clove, minced
- 4 C. homemade chicken broth
- 1 lb. boneless salmon, cubed
- 1 tbsp. low-sodium soy sauce
- 2 tbsp. fresh cilantro, chopped
- Freshly ground black pepper, to taste
- 1 tbsp. fresh lime juice

Instructions:

1) In a large pan heat the oil over medium heat and sauté the onion for about 5 minutes.
2) Add the garlic and sauté for about 1 minute.
3) Stir in the broth and bring to a boil over high heat.
4) Reduce the heat to low and simmer for about 10 minutes.
5) Add the salmon, and soy sauce and cook for about 3-4 minutes.
6) Stir in black pepper, lime juice, and cilantro and serve hot.

Nutrition Information:

Calories per serving: 232; Carbohydrates: 4.1g; Protein: 27.5g; Fat: 11.9g; Sugar: 2.1g; Sodium: 100mg; Fiber: 0.6g

Hearty Beef Stew

Serves: 4

Cooking Time: 1 hour 40 minutes, Preparation Time: 15 minutes

Ingredients:

- 1 1/3 lb. grass-fed chuck roast, trimmed and cubed into 1-inch size
- Salt and freshly ground black pepper, to taste
- 2 tbsp. butter
- 1 yellow onion, finely chopped
- 2 garlic cloves, finely chopped
- 1 C. homemade beef broth
- 1 bay leaf
- ½ tsp. dried thyme, crushed
- ½ tsp. dried rosemary, crushed
- 1 carrot, peeled and thinly sliced
- 4 oz. celery stalks, thinly sliced
- 1 tbsp. fresh lemon juice

Instructions:

1) Season the beef cubes with salt and black pepper.
2) In a Dutch oven, melt the butter over medium-high heat and sear the beef cubes for about 4-5 minutes.
3) Add the onion and garlic and stir to combine.
4) Reduce the heat to medium and cook for about 4-5 minutes.
5) Add the broth, bay leaf and dried herbs and bring to a boil.
6) Reduce the heat to medium-low and simmer for about 45 minutes.
7) Stir in the carrot and celery and simmer for about 30-45 minutes.
8) Stir in lemon juice, salt, and black pepper and remove from the heat.
9) Serve hot.

Nutrition Information:

Calories per serving: 413; Carbohydrates: 5.9g; Protein: 52g; Fat: 18.8g; Sugar: 2.6g; Sodium: 406mg; Fiber: 1.6g

Chilly Night Stew

Serves: 6

Cooking Time: 45 minutes, Preparation Time: 15 minutes

Ingredients:

- 2 tbsp. olive oil
- 2 lb. pork tenderloin, cut into 1-inch cubes
- 1 tbsp. garlic, minced
- 2 tsp. paprika
- ¾ C. homemade chicken broth
- 1 C. sugar-free tomato sauce
- ½ tbsp. Erythritol
- 1 tsp. dried oregano
- 2 dried bay leaves
- 2 tbsp. fresh lemon juice
- Salt and freshly ground black pepper, to taste

Instructions:

1) In a large heavy-bottomed pan, heat the over medium-high heat and cook the pork for about 3-4 minutes or until browned completely.
2) Add the garlic and cook for about 1 minute.
3) Stir in the remaining ingredients and bring to a boil.
4) Reduce the heat to medium-low and simmer, covered for about 30-40 minutes
5) Remove from heat and discard the bay leaves.
6) Serve hot.

Nutrition Information:

Calories per serving: 277; Carbohydrates: 3.6g; Protein: 41g; Fat: 10.4g; Sugar: 2g; Sodium: 785mg; Fiber: 1.1g

Full Meal Chili

Serves: 8

Cooking Time: 2¼ hours, Preparation Time: 15 minutes

Ingredients:

- 2 tbsp. olive oil
- 1 small onion, chopped
- 1 green bell pepper, seeded and chopped
- 4 garlic cloves, minced
- 1 jalapeño pepper, chopped
- 1 tsp. dried thyme, crushed
- 2 tbsp. red chili powder
- 1 tbsp. ground cumin
- 2 lb. lean ground pork
- 2 C. fresh tomatoes, finely chopped
- 4 oz. sugar-free tomato paste
- 1½ tbsp. cacao powder
- 2 C. homemade chicken broth
- 1 C. water
- Salt and freshly ground black pepper, to taste
- ¼ C. cheddar cheese, shredded

Instructions:

1) In a large pan, heat the oil over medium heat and sauté the onion and bell pepper for about 5-7 minutes.

2) Add the garlic, jalapeño pepper, thyme, and spices and sauté for about 1 minute.

3) Add the pork and cook for about 4-5 minutes.

4) Stir in the tomatoes, tomato paste, and cacao powder and cook for about 2 minutes.

5) Add the broth, and water and bring to a boil.

6) Reduce the heat to low and simmer, covered for about 2 hours.

7) Stir in the salt, and black pepper and remove from heat.

8) Top with cheddar cheese and serve hot.

Nutrition Information:

Calories per serving: 326; Carbohydrates: 9.1g; Protein: 23.3g; Fat: 22.9g; Sugar: 4.5g; Sodium: 270mg; Fiber: 2.6g

Award Winning Curry

Serves: 6

Cooking Time: 25 minutes, Preparation Time: 20 minutes

Ingredients:
For Meatballs:
- 1 lb. lean ground pork
- 2 organic eggs, beaten
- 3 tbsp. yellow onion, chopped finely
- ¼ C. fresh parsley leaves, chopped
- ¼ tsp. fresh ginger, minced
- 2 garlic cloves, minced
- 1 jalapeño pepper, seeded and finely chopped
- 1 tsp. Erythritol
- 1 tbsp. red curry paste
- 3 tbsp. olive oil

For Curry:
- 1 yellow onion, chopped
- Salt, to taste
- 2 garlic cloves, minced
- ¼ tsp. fresh ginger, minced
- 2 tbsp. red curry paste
- 1 (14-oz.) can unsweetened coconut milk
- Freshly ground black pepper, to taste
- ¼ C. fresh parsley, chopped

Instructions:
1) For meatballs: in a large bowl, add all the ingredients except oil and mix until well combined.

2) Make small-sized balls from the mixture.

3) In a large skillet, heat the oil over medium heat and cook meatballs for about 3-5 minutes or until golden brown from all sides.

4) With a slotted spoon, transfer the meatballs into a bowl.

5) For curry: in the same skillet, add the onion, and a pinch of salt and sauté for about 4-5 minutes.

6) Add the garlic, and ginger and sauté for about 1 minute.

7) Add the curry paste, and sauté for about 1-2 minutes.

8) Add the coconut milk and meatballs and bring to a gentle simmer.

9) Reduce the heat to low and simmer, covered for about 10-12 minutes.

10) Season with the salt and black pepper and remove from the heat.

11) Top with the parsley and serve hot.

Nutrition Information:

Calories per serving: 444; Carbohydrates: 8.6g; Protein: 17g; Fat: 39.3g; Sugar: 3.3g; Sodium: 192mg; Fiber: 2.2g

Asian Salmon Curry

Serves: 6

Cooking Time: 30 minutes, Preparation Time: 15 minutes

Ingredients:

- 6 (4-oz.) salmon fillets
- 1 tsp. ground turmeric, divided
- Salt, to taste
- 3 tbsp. butter, divided
- 1 yellow onion, chopped finely
- 1 tsp. garlic paste
- 1 tsp. ginger paste
- 3-4 green chilies, halved
- 1 tsp. red chili powder
- ½ tsp. ground cumin
- ½ tsp. ground cinnamon
- ¾ C. plain Greek yogurt, whipped
- ¾ C. water
- 3 tbsp. fresh cilantro, chopped

Instructions:

1) Season each salmon fillet with ½ tsp. of the turmeric and salt.
2) In a large skillet, melt 1 tbsp. of the butter over medium heat and cook the salmon fillets for about 2 minutes per side.
3) Transfer the salmon onto a plate.
4) In the same skillet, melt the remaining butter over medium heat and sauté the onion for about 4-5 minutes.

5) Add the garlic paste, ginger paste, green chilies, remaining turmeric and spices and sauté for about 1 minute.

6) Reduce the heat to medium-low.

7) Slowly, add the yogurt and water, stirring continuously until smooth.

8) Cover the skillet and simmer for about 10-15 minutes or until desired doneness of the sauce.

9) Carefully, add the salmon fillets and simmer for about 5 minutes.

10) Serve hot with the garnishing of cilantro.

Nutrition Information:

Calories per serving: 239; Carbohydrates: 5.5g; Protein: 24.3g; Fat: 13.4g; Sugar: 3.2g; Sodium: 330mg; Fiber: 1.1g

Crowd Pleasing Chicken Parmigiana

Serves: 4

Cooking Time: 26 minutes, Preparation Time: 15 minutes

Ingredients:

- 1 large organic egg, beaten
- ½ C. superfine blanched almond flour
- ¼ C. Parmesan cheese, grated
- ½ tsp. dried parsley
- ½ tsp. paprika
- ½ tsp. garlic powder
- Salt and freshly ground black pepper, to taste
- 4 (6-oz.) grass-fed skinless, boneless chicken breasts, pounded into ½-inch thickness
- ¼ C. olive oil
- 1½ C. sugar-free marinara sauce
- 4 oz. mozzarella cheese, sliced thinly
- 2 tbsp. fresh parsley, chopped

Instructions:

1) Preheat the oven to 375 degrees F.
2) In a shallow dish, place the beaten egg.
3) In another shallow dish, place the almond flour, Parmesan, parsley, spices, salt, and black pepper and mix well.
4) Dip each chicken breast into the beaten egg and then, coat with the flour mixture.
5) In a deep skillet, heat the oil over medium-high heat and fry the chicken breasts for about 3 minutes per side.

6) With a slotted spoon, transfer the chicken breasts onto a paper towel-lined plate to drain.

7) In the bottom of a casserole dish, place about ½ C. of marinara sauce and spread evenly.

8) Arrange the chicken breasts over marinara sauce in a single layer.

9) Top with the remaining marinara sauce, followed by mozzarella cheese slices.

10) Bake for about 20 minutes or until done completely.

11) Remove from the oven and serve hot with the garnishing of fresh parsley.

Nutrition Information:

Calories per serving: 542; Carbohydrates: 9g; Protein: 54.2g; Fat: 33.2g; Sugar: 3.8g; Sodium: 609mg; Fiber: 3.3g

Elegant Chicken Dinner

Serves: 2

Cooking Time: 25 minutes, Preparation Time: 15 minutes

Ingredients:

- 2 (5½ oz.) grass-fed boneless, skinless chicken thighs, cut in half horizontally
- Salt and freshly ground black pepper, to taste
- 1/3 C. almond flour
- 2 tbsp. Parmesan cheese, shredded
- ½ tsp. garlic powder
- 2 tbsp. butter, divided
- 1 tbsp. garlic, minced
- 3 tbsp. capers
- ¼ tsp. red pepper flakes, crushed
- 2 tbsp. fresh lemon juice
- 1 C. homemade chicken broth
- 1/3 C. heavy cream
- 2 tbsp. fresh parsley, chopped

Instructions:

1) Season the chicken thighs evenly with salt and black pepper.
2) In a shallow dish, mix together the flour, parmesan cheese and garlic powder.
3) Coat the chicken thighs with flour mixture and then shake off any excess.
4) In a large skillet, melt 1 tbsp. of the butter over medium-high heat and cook the chicken thighs for about 4-5 minutes per side.
5) With a slotted spoon, place the chicken thighs onto a platter and with a piece of foil, cover them to keep warm.

6) In a bowl, add the capers, garlic, red pepper flakes, lemon juice, and broth and beat until well combined.

7) In the same skillet, melt the remaining butter over medium heat and with a spoon, scrape the brown bits from the bottom.

8) Stir in the capers mixture and cook for about 8-10 minutes or until desired thickness, stirring occasionally.

9) Remove from heat and stir in the heavy cream until smooth.

10) Again, place the skillet over medium heat and cook for about 1 minute.

11) Stir in the cooked chicken and cook for about 1 more minute.

12) Garnish with fresh parsley and serve hot.

Nutrition Information:

Calories per serving: 633; Carbohydrates: 8.6g; Protein: 55g; Fat: 42.3g; Sugar: 1.8g; Sodium: 1000mg; Fiber: 2.9g

Favorite Swiss Chicken Meal

Serves: 4

Cooking Time: 24 minutes, Preparation Time: 20 minutes

Ingredients:

- 4 (6-oz.) grass-fed boneless, skinless chicken breasts, thinly pounded
- 4 thin sugar-free ham slices
- 4 thin Swiss cheese slices
- ½ tsp. paprika
- ½ tsp. garlic powder
- Salt and freshly ground black pepper, to taste
- 1 tbsp. butter, melted
- ½ C. heavy cream
- 2 tbsp. fresh lemon juice
- 1 tbsp. Dijon mustard
- 2 tbsp. fresh parsley, finely chopped

Instructions:

1) Preheat the oven to 400 degrees F.
2) With a sharp knife, cut a pocket in the thickest part of each chicken breast, without cutting all the way through.
3) Place one ham slice into each chicken breast pocket, followed by 1 cheese slice.
4) Fold the chicken over the filling to close.
5) Season each stuffed chicken breast evenly with ¼ tsp. of paprika, ¼ tsp. of garlic powder, salt and black pepper.
6) In a cast iron skillet, melt the butter over medium-high heat and sear the chicken breasts for about 2-2½ minutes per side.

7) Remove from the heat and immediately, transfer the chicken breasts into a casserole dish.

8) Bake for about 10-15 minutes or until chicken is done completely.

9) Meanwhile, for the sauce: in a small pan, add the heavy cream, lemon juice and mustard over high heat and cook for 4-6 minutes, stirring frequently.

10) Stir in the remaining paprika, garlic powder, salt and black pepper and remove from heat.

11) Remove the casserole dish from oven and transfer the chicken breasts onto serving plates.

12) Top each chicken breast with sauce and serve with the garnishing of fresh parsley.

Nutrition Information:

Calories per serving: 559; Carbohydrates: 3.9g; Protein: 62.1g; Fat: 31.5g; Sugar: 0.7g; Sodium: 677mg; Fiber: 0.7g

Dinner Party Casserole

Serves: 6

Cooking Time: 33 minutes, Preparation Time: 15 minutes

Ingredients:

For Chicken Mixture:

- 2 tbsp. butter
- ¼ C. cooked bacon, crumbled
- ½ C. cheddar cheese, shredded
- 4 oz. cream cheese, softened
- ¼ C. heavy whipping cream
- ½ pack ranch seasoning mix
- 2/3 C. homemade chicken broth
- 1½ C. broccoli florets
- 2 C. cooked grass-fed chicken, shredded

For Topping:

- 2 C. cheddar cheese, shredded
- ½ C. cooked bacon, crumbled

Instructions:

1) Preheat the oven to 350 degrees F. Arrange an oven rack in the upper portion of oven.

2) For chicken mixture: in a large ovenproof skillet, melt the butter over low heat.

3) Add the bacon, cheddar cheese, cream cheese, heavy whipping cream, ranch seasoning, and broth and beat until well combined using a wire whisk.

4) Cook for about 5 minutes, stirring frequently.

5) Meanwhile, in a microwave-safe dish, place the broccoli and microwave until desired tenderness is achieved.

6) In the skillet of bacon mixture, add the chicken and broccoli and mix until well combined.

7) Remove the skillet from heat and top with cheddar cheese, followed by bacon.

8) Bake for about 25 minutes.

9) Now, set the oven to broiler.

10) Broil the chicken mixture for about 2-3 minutes or until the cheese is bubbly.

11) Remove from the oven and serve hot.

Nutrition Information:

Calories per serving: 666; Carbohydrates: 3.6g; Protein: 46.5g; Fat: 50.4g; Sugar: 0.8g; Sodium: 1999mg; Fiber: 0.3g

Crispy & Juicy Turkey Breast

Serves: 2

Cooking Time: 1 hour, Preparation Time: 15 minutes

Ingredients:

- ¾ lb. turkey breast
- ½ tsp. dried thyme
- ½ tsp. dried rosemary
- ½ tsp. dried sage
- Salt and freshly ground black pepper, to taste
- 6 large bacon slices

Instructions:

1) Preheat the oven to 350 degrees F. Line a baking sheet with parchment paper.
2) Sprinkle the turkey breast with herb mixture, salt and black pepper.
3) Arrange the bacon slices onto a smooth surface in a row with the slices, pressing against each other.
4) Place the turkey breast on top of the bacon slices.
5) Wrap the end pieces of bacon around the turkey breast first, followed by the middle pieces.
6) Arrange wrapped turkey breast onto the prepared baking sheet.
7) With a piece of foil, cover the turkey breast loosely and bake for about 50 minutes.
8) Remove the foil and bake for about 10 more minutes.
9) Remove from the oven and place the turkey breast onto a platter for about 5-10 minutes before slicing.
10) With a sharp knife, cut the turkey breast into desired size slices and serve.

Nutrition Information:

Calories per serving: 400; Carbohydrates: 1.9g; Protein: 55.4g; Fat: 18.4g; Sugar: 1.6g; Sodium: 1200mg; Fiber: 0.3g

Favorite Italian Dinner

Serves: 4

Cooking Time: 28 minutes, Preparation Time: 15 minutes

Ingredients:

For Mushroom Gravy

- 4 bacon slices, chopped
- 3 tbsp. butter
- 3 garlic cloves, minced
- 1 tsp. dried thyme
- 1½ C. fresh button mushrooms, sliced
- Salt and freshly ground black pepper, to taste
- 7 oz. cream cheese, softened
- ½ C. heavy cream

For Steak

- 4 (6-oz.) grass-fed beef tenderloin filets
- Salt and freshly ground black pepper, to taste
- 3 tbsp. butter

Instructions:

1) For mushroom gravy: heat a large nonstick skillet over medium-high heat and cook the bacon for about 8-10 minutes.
2) With a slotted spoon, transfer the bacon onto a paper towel-lined plate to drain.
3) Discard the bacon grease from the skillet.
4) In the same skillet, melt butter over medium heat and sauté the garlic and thyme for about 1 minute.
5) Stir in the mushrooms, salt, and black pepper and cook for about 5-7 minutes, stirring frequently.

6) Reduce the heat to low and stir in the cream cheese until smooth.

7) Stir in cream and cook for about 2-3 minutes or until heated completely.

8) Meanwhile, rub the beef filets with the salt and black pepper evenly.

9) In a large cast iron skillet, melt the butter over medium heat and cook the filets for about 5-7 minutes per side.

10) Remove the skillet of mushroom gravy from heat and stir in the bacon.

11) Place the filets onto serving plates and serve with the topping of mushroom gravy.

Nutrition Information:

Calories per serving: 895; Carbohydrates: 3.9g; Protein: 65.2g; Fat: 67.9g; Sugar: 0.6g; Sodium: 1040mg; Fiber: 0.4g

Enticing Pork Platter

Serves: 2

Cooking Time: 20 minutes, Preparation Time: 15 minutes

Ingredients:

For Pork Loin:

- 1 tsp. dried thyme
- 1 tsp. paprika
- Salt and freshly ground black pepper, to taste
- 4 (4-oz.) pork loins

For Sauce:

- ½ C. homemade chicken broth
- ¼ C. heavy cream
- 1 tsp. organic apple cider vinegar
- 1 tbsp. fresh lemon juice
- 1 tbsp. mustard
- 2 tbsp. fresh parsley, chopped

Instructions:

1) In a small bowl, mix together the thyme, paprika, salt, and black pepper.
2) Coat each pork loin evenly with the thyme mixture.
3) Heat a lightly greased large pan over high heat and sear the pork loins for about 2-3 minutes per side.
4) With a slotted spoon, transfer the pork loins onto a plate.
5) In the same pan, add the broth, heavy cream, and vinegar over medium heat and bring to a gentle simmer.
6) Add the lemon juice, and mustard and stir to combine.
7) Stir in the cooked pork loins and simmer, covered partially for about 10 minutes.
8) Garnish with parsley and serve hot.

Nutrition Information:

Calories per serving: 647; Carbohydrates: 4.6g; Protein: 65.4g; Fat: 39.4g; Sugar: 0.9g; Sodium: 342mg; Fiber: 1.8g

Hearty Lamb Dinner

Serves: 5

Cooking Time: 20 minutes, Preparation Time: 15 minutes

Ingredients:

- 4 bacon slices, chopped
- 1 lb. grass-fed ground lamb
- ¼ C. green bell pepper, seeded and chopped
- ¼ C. yellow onion, chopped
- 1 tsp. garlic, minced
- 4 C. green cabbage, sliced thinly
- 1 (15-oz.) can sugar-free tomato sauce
- Salt and freshly ground black pepper, to taste

Instructions:

1) Heat a large nonstick skillet over medium heat and cook the bacon for about 5 minutes, stirring occasionally.
2) Add the ground lamb, bell pepper, onion, and garlic and cook for about 7-8 minutes, stirring occasionally.
3) Stir in the cabbage, and tomato sauce and cook, covered for about 5-7 minutes or until desired doneness.
4) Stir in the salt and black pepper and remove from the heat.
5) Serve hot.

Nutrition Information:

Calories per serving: 333; Carbohydrates: 9g; Protein: 36.1g; Fat: 16.6g; Sugar: 5g; Sodium: 1200mg; Fiber: 2.1g

Surprisingly Delicious Salmon

Serves: 4

Cooking Time: 16 minutes, Preparation Time: 15 minutes

Ingredients:

For Salmon:

- 4 (6-oz.) skinless salmon fillets
- Salt and freshly ground black pepper, to taste
- 2 tbsp. fresh lemon juice
- 2 tbsp. olive oil, divided
- 1 tbsp. unsalted butter

For Filling:

- 4 oz. cream cheese, softened
- ¼ C. Parmesan cheese, grated finely
- 4 oz. frozen spinach thawed and squeezed
- 2 tsp. garlic, minced
- Salt and freshly ground black pepper, to taste

Instructions:

1) Season each salmon fillet with salt and black pepper and then, drizzle with the lemon juice and 1 tbsp. of the oil evenly.
2) Arrange the salmon fillets onto a smooth surface.
3) With a sharp knife, cut a pocket into each salmon fillet about ¾ of the way through, being careful not to cut all the way.
4) For filling: in a bowl, place the cream cheese, Parmesan cheese, spinach, garlic, salt and black pepper and mix well.
5) Place about 1-2 tbsp. of the spinach mixture into each salmon pocket and spread evenly.

6) Heat the remaining oil and butter and in a skillet over medium-high heat and cook the salmon fillets for about 6-8 minutes per side.

7) Remove the salmon fillets from the heat and transfer onto the serving plates.

8) Serve immediately.

Nutrition Information:

Calories per serving: 438; Carbohydrates: 2.4g; Protein: 38.1g; Fat: 31.7g; Sugar: 0.4g; Sodium: 285mg; Fiber: 0.7g

Mid-Week Dinner Casserole

Serves: 5

Cooking Time: 27 minutes, Preparation Time: 15 minutes

Ingredients:

- 2 tbsp. olive oil
- 15 oz. broccoli, chopped
- 6 scallions, chopped
- 2 tbsp. small capers
- Salt and freshly ground black pepper, to taste
- 1¼ C. heavy whipping cream
- 1 tbsp. dried parsley
- 1 tbsp. Dijon mustard
- 25 oz. grouper fillets, cut into bite-sized pieces
- 3 oz. chilled butter, chopped

Instructions:

1) Preheat the oven to 400 degrees F. Grease a baking dish.
2) In a skillet, heat the olive oil over medium-high heat and cook the broccoli for about 5 minutes, until golden and soft.
3) Stir in the scallions, capers, salt and black pepper and cook for about 1-2 minutes.
4) Meanwhile, place the whipping cream, parsley and mustard in a bowl and mix well.
5) Remove the skillet of broccoli mixture from the heat and place the broccoli mixture into the prepared baking dish evenly.
6) Top with the grouper pieces and gently, press into the broccoli mixture.
7) Place the whipping cream mixture on top evenly.

8) Spread the butter pieces on top evenly.

9) Bake for about 19-20 minutes or until desired doneness of the fish.

10) Remove the baking dish from the oven and let it cool for about 5 minutes before serving.

Nutrition Information:

Calories per serving: 479; Carbohydrates: 8.3g; Protein: 39.8g; Fat: 32.8g; Sugar: 2g; Sodium: 819mg; Fiber: 3g

21 Days Meal Plan for Meal Prep

Day 1

Satisfying Breakfast Smoothie

(Calories per serving: 392; Carbohydrates: 6.2g; Protein: 24.3g; Fat: 28.9g; Sugar: 4g; Sodium: 100mg; Fiber: 0.3g)

Lunch: Savory Zucchini Cake

(Calories per serving: 140; Carbohydrates: 3.3g; Protein: 8.9g; Fat: 10.7g; Sugar: 1.6g; Sodium: 227mg; Fiber: 1g)

Dinner: Filling Shrimp Salad

(Calories per serving: 303; Carbohydrates: 10.5g; Protein: 24.3g; Fat: 18.5g; Sugar: 2.5g; Sodium: 420mg; Fiber: 4g)

Day 2

Breakfast: Eggy Flavored Crepes

(Calories per serving: 283; Carbohydrates: 3.8g; Protein: 12.9g; Fat: 24.3g; Sugar: 0.8g; Sodium: 274mg; Fiber: 1.6g)

Lunch: Thanksgiving Favorite Burgers

(Calories per serving: 544; Carbohydrates: 9.4g; Protein: 39.3g; Fat: 44.5g; Sugar: 3.3g; Sodium: 900mg; Fiber: 3.4g)

Dinner: Mexican Chicken Soup

(Calories per serving: 345; Carbohydrates: 2.9g; Protein: 32.2g; Fat: 22.1g; Sugar: 1g; Sodium: 857mg; Fiber: 0.1g)

Day 3

Breakfast: Aromatic Cinnamon Bread

(Calories per serving: 140; Carbohydrates: 2.3g; Protein: 3.1g; Fat: 13.5g; Sugar: 0.5g; Sodium: 231mg; Fiber: 1.3g)

Lunch: Dairy-Free Creamy Soup

(Calories per serving: 227; Carbohydrates: 9.4g; Protein: 4.5g; Fat: 20.4g; Sugar: 1g; Sodium: 417mg; Fiber: 6.8g)

Dinner: Ultimate Steak Salad

(Calories per serving: 521; Carbohydrates: 9g; Protein: 39.5g; Fat: 36.3g; Sugar: 5g; Sodium: 279mg; Fiber: 2.4g)

Day 4

Breakfast: Authentic Belgian Waffles

(Calories per serving: 335; Carbohydrates: 9.5g; Protein: 13.6g; Fat: 27.3g; Sugar: 0.7g; Sodium: 397mg; Fiber: 4.5g)

Lunch: Gourmet Shrimp Tacos

(Calories per serving: 841; Carbohydrates: 7.5g; Protein: 31.6g; Fat: 76.7g; Sugar: 1.1g; Sodium: 929mg; Fiber: 3.7g)

Dinner: Beef Taco Soup

(Calories per serving: 281; Carbohydrates: 6g; Protein: 19.2g; Fat: 19.8g; Sugar: 2.9g; Sodium: 844mg; Fiber: 1.3g)

Day 5

Breakfast: Fall Morning Porridge

(Calories per serving: 113; Carbohydrates: 8g; Protein: 3.7g; Fat: 7.6g; Sugar: 1g; Sodium: 303mg; Fiber: 3.8g)

Lunch: Refreshingly Tasty Meatballs

(Calories per serving: 236; Carbohydrates: 5.5g; Protein: 19.6g; Fat: 15.7g; Sugar: 1g; Sodium: 172mg; Fiber: 3.2g)

Dinner: Enticing Pork Platter

(Calories per serving: 647; Carbohydrates: 4.6g; Protein: 65.4g; Fat: 39.4g; Sugar: 0.9g; Sodium: 342mg; Fiber: 1.8g)

Day 6

Breakfast: Delicious Pancakes

(Calories per serving: 165; Carbohydrates: 7.7g; Protein: 19.2g; Fat: 6.3g; Sugar: 0.7g; Sodium: 468mg; Fiber: 3.4g)

Lunch: Rich Cauliflower Soup

(Calories per serving: 121; Carbohydrates: 8.3g; Protein: 5.5g; Fat: 7.7g; Sugar: 3.6g; Sodium: 676mg; Fiber: 2.7g)

Dinner: Crowd Pleasing Chicken Parmigiana

Calories per serving: 542; Carbohydrates: 9g; Protein: 54.2g; Fat: 33.2g; Sugar: 3.8g; Sodium: 609mg; Fiber: 3.3g

Day 7

Breakfast: Classic Sausage Frittata

(Calories per serving: 131; Carbohydrates: 2.2g; Protein: 9.5g; Fat: 9.7g; Sugar: 0.7g; Sodium: 282mg; Fiber: 0.9g)

Lunch: Crunchy Chicken Salad Wraps

(Calories per serving: 392; Carbohydrates: 5.4g; Protein: 35.3g; Fat: 24.5g; Sugar: 2.8g; Sodium: 252mg; Fiber: 2.1g)

Dinner: Hearty Lamb Dinner

(Calories per serving: 333; Carbohydrates: 9g; Protein: 36.1g; Fat: 16.6g; Sugar: 5g; Sodium: 1200mg; Fiber: 2.1g)

Day 8

(Calories per serving: 179; Carbohydrates: 4.3g; Protein: 6g; Fat: 15.6g; Sugar: 0.6g; Sodium: 317mg; Fiber: 1.7g)

Lunch: Vibrant Tomato Soup

(Calories per serving: 113; Carbohydrates: 9.4g; Protein: 5.1g; Fat: 2.7g; Sugar: 5g; Sodium: 553mg; Fiber: 6.7g)

Dinner: Elegant Chicken Dinner

(Calories per serving: 633; Carbohydrates: 8.6g; Protein: 55g; Fat: 42.3g; Sugar: 1.8g; Sodium: 1000mg; Fiber: 2.9g)

Day 9

Breakfast: Fluffy Broccoli Omelet

(Calories per serving: 244; Carbohydrates: 6.9g; Protein: 16.5g; Fat: 17.4g; Sugar: 1.9g; Sodium: 280mg; Fiber: 1.9g)

Lunch: Crunchy Lunch Salad

(Calories per serving: 195; Carbohydrates: 10g; Protein: 13.7g; Fat: 10.9g; Sugar: 4g; Sodium: 838mg; Fiber: 1.8g)

Dinner: Chilly Night Stew

(Calories per serving: 277; Carbohydrates: 3.6g; Protein: 41g; Fat: 10.4g; Sugar: 2g; Sodium: 785mg; Fiber: 1.1g)

Day 10

Breakfast: Overnight Porridge

(Calories per serving: 265; Carbohydrates: 6.5g; Protein: 14.1g; Fat: 20.4g; Sugar: 0.1g; Sodium: 78mg; Fiber: 5.7g)

Lunch: Flavor Packed Meatballs

(Calories per serving: 183; Carbohydrates: 4.6g; Protein: 24.1g; Fat: 7.4g; Sugar: 2.3g; Sodium: 545mg; Fiber: 1.3g)

Dinner: Surprisingly Delicious Salmon

(Calories per serving: 438; Carbohydrates: 2.4g; Protein: 38.1g; Fat: 31.7g; Sugar: 0.4g; Sodium: 285mg; Fiber: 0.7g)

Day 11

Breakfast: Southwest Tofu Scramble

(Calories per serving: 168; Carbohydrates: 6.5g; Protein: 16.2g; Fat: 10.6g; Sugar: 2.8g; Sodium: 66mg; Fiber: 1.6g)

Lunch: Timeless Luncheon Scallops

(Calories per serving: 362; Carbohydrates: 2.1g; Protein: 40g; Fat: 17.5g; Sugar: 0g; Sodium: 575mg; Fiber: 1g)

Dinner: Full Meal Chili

(Calories per serving: 326; Carbohydrates: 9.1g; Protein: 23.3g; Fat: 22.9g; Sugar: 4.5g; Sodium: 270mg; Fiber: 2.6g)

Day 12

Breakfast: Best Homemade Granola

(Calories per serving: 156; Carbohydrates: 7.2g; Protein: 5.4g; Fat: 13.5g; Sugar: 0.6g; Sodium: 66mg; Fiber: 3.9g)

Lunch: Appealing Zucchini Boats

(Calories per serving: 390; Carbohydrates: 10g; Protein: 32.5g; Fat: 25.3g; Sugar: 5g; Sodium: 445mg; Fiber: 2.9g)

Dinner: Easy-Going Pork Salad

(Calories per serving: 292; Carbohydrates: 4.8g; Protein: 37.7g; Fat: 13.4g; Sugar: 2.24g; Sodium: 372mg; Fiber: 1.8g)

Day 13

Breakfast: Perfect Broccoli Muffins

(Calories per serving: 205; Carbohydrates: 2.5g; Protein: 12.2g; Fat: 16.7g; Sugar: 0.9g; Sodium: 210mg; Fiber: 0.5g)

Lunch: Thai Salad Wraps

(Calories per serving: 280; Carbohydrates: 7.4g; Protein: 24.2g; Fat: 16.1g; Sugar: 3.5g; Sodium: 726mg; Fiber: 1.5g)

Dinner: Mid-Week Dinner Casserole

(Calories per serving: 479; Carbohydrates: 8.3g; Protein: 39.8g; Fat: 32.8g; Sugar: 2g; Sodium: 819mg; Fiber: 3g)

Day 14

Breakfast: Crustless Quiche

(Calories per serving: 352; Carbohydrates: 6.1g; Protein: 22.1g; Fat: 26.9g; Sugar: 1.1g; Sodium: 1011mg; Fiber: 1.8g)

Lunch: High Protein Lunch

(Calories per serving: 162; Carbohydrates: 6.2g; Protein: 8g; Fat: 13.1g; Sugar: 1.8g; Sodium: 94mg; Fiber: 2.3g)

Dinner: Favorite Italian Dinner

(Calories per serving: 895; Carbohydrates: 3.9g; Protein: 65.2g; Fat: 67.9g; Sugar: 0.6g; Sodium: 1040mg; Fiber: 0.4g)

Day 15

Breakfast: Protein Rich Smoothie

(Calories per serving: 460; Carbohydrates: 9g; Protein: 25.3g; Fat: 34.5g; Sugar: 5g; Sodium: 332mg; Fiber: 2.5g)

Lunch: Unstuffed Cabbage Casserole

(Calories per serving: 273; Carbohydrates: 9g; Protein: 6.2g; Fat: 15.4g; Sugar: 4g; Sodium: 313mg; Fiber: 3.4g)

Dinner: Favorite Swiss Chicken Meal

(Calories per serving: 559; Carbohydrates: 3.9g; Protein: 62.1g; Fat: 31.5g; Sugar: 0.7g; Sodium: 677mg; Fiber: 0.7g)

Day 16

Breakfast: Staple Breakfast Bread

(Calories per serving: 169; Carbohydrates: 4.4g; Protein: 5.7g; Fat: 15.4g; Sugar: 0.7g; Sodium: 89mg; Fiber: 2.4g)

Lunch: Pool-Side Lunch Burgers

(Calories per serving: 230; Carbohydrates: 4.4g; Protein: 32.5g; Fat: 8.6g; Sugar: 1.2g; Sodium: 325mg; Fiber: 1.1g)

Dinner: Crispy & Juicy Turkey Breast

(Calories per serving: 400; Carbohydrates: 1.9g; Protein: 55.4g; Fat: 18.4g; Sugar: 1.6g; Sodium: 1200mg; Fiber: 0.3g)

Day 17

Breakfast: Stuffed Avocado Cups

(Calories per serving: 280; Carbohydrates: 9.2g; Protein: 8.5g; Fat: 24.7g; Sugar: 0.9g; Sodium: 149mg; Fiber: 6.8g)

Lunch: Creamy Shrimp Salad

(Calories per serving: 429; Carbohydrates: 4.1g; Protein: 34.8g; Fat: 29.3g; Sugar: 0.8g; Sodium: 648mg; Fiber: 0.7g)

Dinner: Dinner Party Casserole

(Calories per serving: 666; Carbohydrates: 3.6g; Protein: 46.5g; Fat: 50.4g; Sugar: 0.8g; Sodium: 1999mg; Fiber: 0.3g)

Day 18

Breakfast: Savory Herbed Waffles

(Calories per serving: 243; Carbohydrates: 5.3g; Protein: 14.1g; Fat: 19.2g; Sugar: 1.1g; Sodium: 288mg; Fiber: 2.1g)

Lunch: Marinated Tomato Salad

(Calories per serving: 143; Carbohydrates: 9g; Protein: 2.1g; Fat: 11.8g; Sugar: 5g; Sodium: 63mg; Fiber: 2.5g)

Dinner: Award Winning Curry

(Calories per serving: 444; Carbohydrates: 8.6g; Protein: 17g; Fat: 39.3g; Sugar: 3.3g; Sodium: 192mg; Fiber: 2.2g)

Day 19

Breakfast: Sweet & Zesty Muffin

(Calories per serving: 214; Carbohydrates: 2.8g; Protein: 5.9g; Fat: 19.9g; Sugar: 1.2g; Sodium: 278mg; Fiber: 1.1g)

Lunch: Brilliant Cheesy Broccoli

(Calories per serving: 359; Carbohydrates: 8g; Protein: 12.2g; Fat: 32.2g; Sugar: 2.1g; Sodium: 430mg; Fiber: 3g)

Dinner: Omega-3 Rich Soup

(Calories per serving: 232; Carbohydrates: 4.1g; Protein: 27.5g; Fat: 11.9g; Sugar: 2.1g; Sodium: 100mg; Fiber: 0.6g)

Day 20

(Calories per serving: 167; Carbohydrates: 6g; Protein: 3.8g; Fat: 15.3g; Sugar: 0.8g; Sodium: 4mg; Fiber: 4g)

Lunch: Juiciest Beef Burgers

(Calories per serving: 338; Carbohydrates: 0.7g; Protein: 54g; Fat: 11.9g; Sugar: 0.1g; Sodium: 205mg; Fiber: 0.3g)

Dinner: Asian Salmon Curry

(Calories per serving: 239; Carbohydrates: 5.5g; Protein: 24.3g; Fat: 13.4g; Sugar: 3.2g; Sodium: 330mg; Fiber: 1.1g)

Day 21

Breakfast: Mediterranean Breakfast

(Calories per serving: 174; Carbohydrates: 4.3g; Protein: 11.9g; Fat: 13g; Sugar: 0.9g; Sodium: 287mg; Fiber: 1.9g)

Lunch: Fabulous Salmon Salad

(Calories per serving: 279; Carbohydrates: 10g; Protein: 14.6g; Fat: 21.5g; Sugar: 4.2g; Sodium: 1000mg; Fiber: 4.4g)

Dinner: Hearty Beef Stew

(Calories per serving: 413; Carbohydrates: 5.9g; Protein: 52g; Fat: 18.8g; Sugar: 2.6g; Sodium: 406mg; Fiber: 1.6g)

Made in the
USA
Middletown, DE